BETWEEN NOW AND NOT YET
A YEAR OF DEVOTIONALS AND HARD-DAY PRAYERS

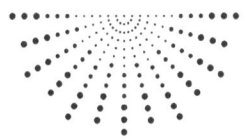

THE MIND OF MALACHI

Between Now and Not Yet

A Year of Devotionals and Hard-Day Prayers

By The Mind of Malachi

Published by The Legacy Group

© 2025 The Mind of Malachi

All rights reserved.

No part of this book may be reproduced, stored in a retrieval system, or transmitted in any form or by any means electronic, mechanical, photocopying, recording, or otherwise without the prior written permission of the publisher, except in the case of brief quotations used in reviews or critical articles.

This book is a blend of truth and fiction. Some events are inspired by real experiences, while others have been dramatized, altered, or entirely imagined for storytelling purposes. Names, characters, places, and identifying details have been changed to protect the privacy of individuals. Any resemblance to actual persons, living or dead, or to actual events is coincidental or used fictitiously. While inspired by real experiences, the actions and events described are fictionalized and do not reflect endorsements or actual practices of any persons or organizations mentioned.

First Edition - November 2025

Printed in the United States of America

Cover & Interior design by The Mind of Malachi

The Legacy Group

Houston, Texas

ISBN (Paperback): 978-1-970955-99-6

ISBN (eBook): 978-1-970955-98-9

ISBN (Hardback): 978-1-970955-97-2

SCRIPTURE CREDITS

Unless otherwise indicated, all Scripture quotations are taken from the Holy Bible, New International Version®, NIV®. Copyright © 1973, 1978, 1984, 2011 by Biblica, Inc.™ Used by permission of Zondervan. All rights reserved worldwide. www.zondervan.com. The "NIV" and "New International Version" are trademarks registered in the United States Patent and Trademark Office by Biblica, Inc.™

And for every single person who has ever felt forgotten: You're not.

CONTENTS

Introduction ix

PART I

WEEK 1: Starting Right Where You Are 3
WEEK 2: You Are Not Forgotten 10
WEEK 3: You Are Not Unfinished 16
WEEK 4: Your Singleness Is Not Punishment 22
WEEK 5: This Is Not a Waiting Room 29
WEEK 6: Fully Loved, Fully Seen, Fully Enough 36
WEEK 7: When Everyone Else's Story Feels Better Than Yours 43
WEEK 8: God's Design for This Season 50
WEEK 9: You Are Not Half a Person 56
WEEK 10: Breaking the "Incomplete" Narrative 62
WEEK 11: His Love Doesn't Depend on Your Relationship Status 68
WEEK 12: The Gift of Undivided Devotion 74
WEEK 13: Anchored in Christ, Not Circumstance 80
WEEK 14: The Wounds That Still Ache 87
WEEK 15: Forgiving the One Who Hurt You 93
WEEK 16: Forgiving Yourself 99
WEEK 17: Breaking Unhealthy Relationship Patterns 106
WEEK 18: When Past Rejection Still Speaks 112
WEEK 19: Guarding Your Heart Without Hardening It 118
WEEK 20: Honoring Your Body as Sacred 124
WEEK 21: The Struggle With Sexual Purity 130
WEEK 22: When Desire Feels Like a Burden 136
WEEK 23: Healing From Toxic Relationships 142
WEEK 24: Letting Go of What Could Have Been 148
WEEK 25: When You Keep Choosing the Wrong Person 154
WEEK 26: Becoming Whole, Not Just Looking for Completion 160
WEEK 27: You Were Made for More Than Marriage 166
WEEK 29: Stewardship of Your Single Season 172
WEEK 30: Building Kingdom Community 178
WEEK 31: Serving From Overflow, Not Emptiness 184

WEEK 33: Being Present Where God Has You	190
WEEK 34: When Your Purpose Feels Unclear	196
WEEK 35: Living Fully, Not Half-Alive	201
WEEK 36: The Freedom to Say Yes	207
WEEK 37: The Courage to Pursue Dreams Now	212
WEEK 38: You Don't Need Permission to Thrive	217
WEEK 39: Making the Most of This Season	222
WEEK 40: Contentment and Anticipation Together	227
WEEK 41: Surrendering Your Timeline to God	233
WEEK 42: Trusting His Timing When It Doesn't Make Sense	239
WEEK 43: Preparing for Whatever Comes Next	244
WEEK 44: Praying for Your Future (Marriage or Singleness)	249
WEEK 46: When Waiting Feels Endless	254
WEEK 47: Hope That Doesn't Disappoint	259
WEEK 48: Believing God's Promises Over Your Feelings	264
WEEK 51: Looking Ahead With Faith	270
WEEK 52: The End of a Year, The Beginning of Forever	275

PART II

Part I
CALENDAR HARD DAYS

NEW YEAR'S EVE/DAY	285
YOUR BIRTHDAY	287
VALENTINE'S DAY	289
MOTHER'S DAY/FATHER'S DAY	291
WEDDING SEASON	293
THANKSGIVING	295
CHRISTMAS	297

Part II
LIFE EVENT HARD DAYS

WHEN YOUR EX GETS ENGAGED/MARRIED	301
WHEN YOUR YOUNGER SIBLING/FRIEND MARRIES FIRST: The Unexpected Sting	303
AFTER A DEVASTATING BREAKUP: When Hope Just Died	305
WHEN YOU'RE THE LAST SINGLE FRIEND: Population: You	307

WHEN THE DATES KEEP GOING NOWHERE	309
WHEN YOUR BIOLOGICAL CLOCK IS SCREAMING	311
Chapter 1	313
Chapter 2	315
WHEN YOU'RE TIRED OF PRAYING	317

Part III
CHURCH & COMMUNITY HARD DAYS

WHEN CHURCH FEELS LIKE COUPLES CLUB	323
WHEN SOMEONE SAYS "YOU'RE TOO PICKY"	325
WHEN SOMEONE SAYS "JUST TRUST GOD'S TIMING"	327
WHEN SEXUAL TEMPTATION OVERWHELMS	329
WHEN YOU WONDER IF SOMETHING'S WRONG WITH YOU	331
About the Author	333
ALSO BY THE Mind of Malachi	335
Acknowledgments	337

INTRODUCTION

You picked up this book for a reason.

Maybe you're exhausted from hearing "God's timing is perfect" from people who got married at twenty-three. Maybe you're tired of pretending you're fine when everyone around you is pairing off and moving on. Maybe you're wondering if there's something fundamentally wrong with you that no one will say out loud.

Maybe you're just tired.

This book won't tell you that singleness is easy. It won't promise that if you pray harder and trust more, everything will work out the way you hope. It won't pretend that faith makes waiting painless.

Because life doesn't work that way. Faith doesn't work that way. And pretending otherwise doesn't help anyone.

What this book will tell you is the truth:

You are not forgotten. You are not unfinished. You are not being punished.

Your singleness isn't God withholding good things from you. It's not a holding pattern until "real life" begins. It's not proof that you're too broken, too picky, or too anything.

This is your life. Right now. Today. And God is with you in it.

The Journey Ahead

This is a year with someone who understands.

Fifty-two weeks of devotionals and prayers that don't pretend waiting is easy. Each week meets you where you are, no matter when you start, no matter what you're carrying.

Monday brings a devotional that reframes the lies you've been believing. Tuesday through Saturday give you five prayers for the days when you don't have words of your own. Sunday offers space to reflect, declare truth over yourself, and carry Scripture into the week ahead.

You don't have to start in January. You don't have to wait for the "right time." Week 1 begins whenever you open this book.

This isn't a curriculum to complete. It's a companion for the journey, one that refuses to sugarcoat the struggle but also refuses to let you believe the lies.

Our Prayer for You

We're praying that this year transforms how you see yourself, your season, and God's love for you.

That you'll stop measuring your worth by your relationship status and start seeing yourself the way God does. Fully loved. Fully seen. Fully enough.

That you'll stop putting your life on hold and start living fully in the season you're actually in.

That you'll heal wounds you've been ignoring, break patterns you've been repeating, and build a life worth living right now.

That you'll find hope that doesn't depend on outcomes. Peace that holds even when nothing makes sense. Faith that trusts God's character more than your timeline.

We're not promising you'll be married by the end of this year. We're not guaranteeing your circumstances will look different. We can't tell you when or how your story will unfold.

But we are praying that you'll be different. That you'll walk through this year and come out stronger, more whole, more anchored in Christ than you were when you started.

That's what this book is for.

The Hard Days

Life doesn't pause for devotionals.

You're going to have weeks where you're doing fine, following along, growing. And then Valentine's Day hits. Or your ex gets engaged. Or you attend another wedding alone. Or it's 2 a.m. and the loneliness feels unbearable.

That's why Part Two of this book exists.

At the back, you'll find twenty-one prayers for the hardest days, organized by category so you can find exactly what you need when life knocks the wind out of you. They're shorter, more immediate, designed to meet you in crisis.

Calendar Hard Days for the dates that sting every year. Life Event Hard Days for the moments that ambush you. Church and Community Hard Days for the wounds that come from people who should be safe.

Use them whenever you need them. Then come back to wherever you are in the fifty-two weeks and keep going.

A Word Before You Begin

You might be starting this book in the middle of heartbreak. You might be starting it after years of contentment that suddenly turned into loneliness. You might be starting it because someone handed it to you and said, "I think you need this."

Wherever you are, however you got here, you're in the right place.

God sees you. Not as a project to fix or a problem to solve, but as His beloved. Fully loved. Fully seen. Fully enough.

Right now.

Not when you meet someone. Not when you "get it together." Not when your life looks the way you thought it would.

Right now.

This year is going to be hard sometimes. Growth always is. But you're not walking through it alone.

Let's begin.

PART I

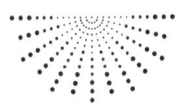

WEEK 1: STARTING RIGHT WHERE YOU ARE

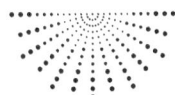

MONDAY DEVOTIONAL

You don't need to have it all together to start.

That's the first lie most of us believe, that we need to be in a "better place" emotionally, spiritually, or mentally before we can really begin working on ourselves. That once we're less angry, less hurt, less exhausted, then we can start growing.

But here's the truth: God meets you exactly where you are.

Not where you think you should be. Not where other people are. Not where you were five years ago or hope to be five years from now.

Right here. Right now. In the middle of whatever mess you're carrying.

Maybe you're starting this book because you're desperate. Maybe you're starting because someone who loves you suggested it. Maybe you're starting because you're tired of feeling stuck and you don't know what else to do.

It doesn't matter.

What matters is that you're here.

You showed up.

And that's enough to begin.

There's a moment in Scripture that doesn't get talked about enough. In Mark 9, a father brings his demon-possessed son to Jesus, begging for help. And Jesus says, "Everything is possible for one who believes."

The father's response is raw and honest:

"I do believe; help me overcome my unbelief!" (Mark 9:24, NIV)

He didn't have perfect faith. He didn't have it all figured out. He showed up with doubt and desperation tangled together and said, essentially, "I'm here, but I'm a mess. Help me."

And Jesus didn't send him away to "work on his faith" first. He healed the son right there.

That's where you are today.

You might believe God loves you, but also wonder why He hasn't brought someone into your life yet. You might trust His timing, but also feel furious that His timing looks nothing like what you hoped. You might know, intellectually, that you're not forgotten, but feel, emotionally, completely invisible.

All of that is okay.

You don't need to clean up your doubts, package your questions neatly, or pretend you're more okay than you are.

You just need to show up.

God isn't afraid of your mess. He isn't intimidated by your anger, your confusion, or your exhaustion. He isn't waiting for you to get yourself together before He'll meet with you.

He's already here.

Right where you are.

So take a breath. You don't need to have next week figured out, let alone the next fifty-two. You don't need to know how this story ends or when things will change.

You just need to be here today.

And that's exactly where we're going to start.

MONDAY PRAYER

God, I'm here.

I'm not sure I have the energy for this, but I'm showing up anyway. I'm tired of feeling stuck. I'm tired of feeling like everyone else is moving forward while I'm standing still. I don't know if this year is going to change anything, but I'm willing to try.

Meet me here. I'm not pretending I have it all together, because I don't. I'm not pretending I'm not angry or confused or exhausted, because I am. But I'm here. And I'm asking You to meet me in this exact moment, in this exact mess.

Help me believe that showing up is enough. That I don't need to be perfect to start. That You see me, right here, right now, and that You're not disappointed.

I'm starting this journey today, and I'm trusting that You'll walk it with me.

In Jesus' name, Amen.

TUESDAY PRAYER

Father, I've been carrying so much on my own.

I've been trying to figure out my life, manage my feelings, and navigate this season without leaning on You the way I should. I've been functioning, surviving, going through the motions, but I haven't been truly depending on You.

I don't want to do that anymore.

This year, I'm giving You permission to lead. I'm giving You my questions, my frustrations, my timeline, my expectations, all of it. I don't know what's going to change, but I'm asking You to change me. Not because I'm broken, but because I want to be whole.

Teach me what it means to be fully Yours. Teach me what it means to rest in Your love instead of striving for everyone else's approval.

I'm ready to stop carrying this alone.

In Jesus' name, Amen.

WEDNESDAY PRAYER

God, I need You to silence the voices.

The ones that tell me I'm falling behind. The ones that say something must be wrong with me. The ones that compare my life to everyone else's highlight reel and tell me I'm losing.

Those voices are loud. And some days, I believe them.

But I know they're not from You. You don't measure my worth by my relationship status. You don't rank my value based on whether someone has chosen me. You don't look at my life and see failure.

Help me hear Your voice above all the others. Remind me who I am in Your eyes. Anchor me in the truth that I am loved, seen, and enough, not because of what I have, but because of who You are.

Drown out the lies with Your truth.

In Jesus' name, Amen.

THURSDAY PRAYER

Lord, I'm afraid of wasting time.

I look at my life and wonder if I'm doing this wrong. If I'm missing opportunities. If I'm too guarded or not guarded enough. If I should be putting myself out there more or protecting my heart better.

I'm afraid that while I'm waiting, life is passing me by.

But I don't want fear to dictate my decisions anymore. I don't want anxiety to be the loudest voice in the room. I want to trust that You're not letting me waste anything, that every season, even this one, has purpose.

Help me stop second-guessing every choice. Help me trust that You're guiding me, even when I can't see the path clearly. Give me peace that this season, however long it lasts, is not wasted time.

You're working, even when I can't see it.

In Jesus' name, Amen.

FRIDAY PRAYER

Father, I don't know where this is going.

I don't know if I'll be single next year or in five years or forever. I don't know if someone is coming or if this is the life You've called me to. And honestly, that uncertainty feels suffocating sometimes.

But I'm choosing to trust You today. Not because I have answers, but because I believe You see the full picture. I believe You know what I need better than I do. And I believe that even when I can't see the road ahead, You're already there.

So I'm giving You today. Just today. I'm not going to spiral about tomorrow or obsess over next year. I'm just going to trust You with the next twenty-four hours.

Help me take this one day at a time.

In Jesus' name, Amen.

SATURDAY PRAYER

God, thank You for not giving up on me.

Thank You for meeting me in the mess. Thank You for not requiring me to be perfect before You'll love me. Thank You for pursuing me even when I've been distant, doubtful, or difficult.

This week, I showed up. Some days it was barely, but I did it. And somehow, that was enough for You.

As I move into next week, help me carry that truth with me. Help me remember that Your love isn't conditional on my performance. That You're not waiting for me to earn Your presence.

You're already here. And that changes everything.

In Jesus' name, Amen.

SUNDAY REFLECTION

Reflect:

- What made you pick up this book today? What are you hoping will change this year?

- What does it feel like to know that God meets you exactly where you are, not where you think you should be?

Declare:

- I don't need to have it all together to begin.

- God meets me exactly where I am.

- Showing up is enough.

> Carry This: "Come to me, all you who are weary and burdened, and I will give you rest.", Matthew 11:28 (NIV)

SUNDAY PRAYER

God, I showed up this week.

I didn't have it all together. I didn't know what I was doing. But I started. And somehow, that was enough for You.

As I move into this next week, help me keep showing up. Help me keep choosing to be present, to be honest, to bring You what I have instead of waiting until I'm "ready."

This journey is just beginning. And I'm grateful You're walking it with me.

In Jesus' name, Amen.

WEEK 2: YOU ARE NOT FORGOTTEN

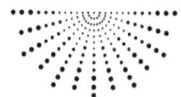

MONDAY DEVOTIONAL

There's a specific kind of pain that comes with feeling forgotten.

It's not dramatic. It's not the kind of hurt that makes headlines or gets sympathy from others. It's quiet. Persistent. The kind that sits in your chest at 2 a.m. when everyone else is asleep and you're wondering if God actually sees you.

You watch other people's prayers get answered. You see relationships form, engagements announced, weddings planned. You hear testimonies about God's perfect timing and divine appointments, and you think, "What about me? Did He forget about my story?"

Let me tell you something with absolute certainty: He didn't.

In Psalm 139, David writes something that should fundamentally reshape how we understand God's attention:

> "You have searched me, Lord, and you know me. You know when I sit and when I rise; you perceive my thoughts from afar" (Psalm 139:1-2, NIV).

Not "You knew me once." Not "You'll know me eventually."

You know me. Present tense. Right now.

God isn't distracted by the seven billion other people on this planet. He isn't overwhelmed by prayer requests or too busy managing the universe to notice your life. He sees you. Specifically. Personally. Completely.

Every morning you wake up alone and wish you didn't, He sees.

Every wedding you attend with a smile plastered on while your heart aches, He sees.

Every time you scroll past another engagement photo and feel the sting of being left behind, He sees.

He's not ignoring you. He's not punishing you. He's not waiting for you to prove something before He'll act.

He sees you. He knows you. And He has not forgotten your name.

The Enemy wants you to believe that silence means absence. That unanswered prayers mean God doesn't care. That delayed timing means you've been overlooked.

But God's silence is not His absence. His timing is not His neglect.

You are seen. You are known. You are not forgotten.

And that truth stands whether your circumstances change tomorrow or ten years from now.

MONDAY PRAYER

God, sometimes I feel invisible.

I know in my head that You see me, but my heart doesn't always believe it. When I watch everyone else's lives move forward and mine feels stuck, it's hard not to think You've forgotten about me.

Remind me today that Your attention isn't divided. That You're not distracted by everyone else's needs. That You see me, specifically, personally, completely.

Help me believe that I matter to You. Not because of what I accomplish or who I'm with, but simply because I'm Yours.

I don't need You to change my circumstances today. I just need to know You haven't forgotten me.

In Jesus' name, Amen.

TUESDAY PRAYER

Father, I'm tired of feeling overlooked.

By potential partners. By married friends who don't know how to include me anymore. By a world that seems designed for couples and families.

But more than anything, I'm afraid of being overlooked by You.

I see You answer other people's prayers, for relationships, for families, for the things I've been begging You for, and I wonder why not me. What makes them different? What am I doing wrong?

Silence those questions. Replace them with truth. You have not forgotten me. You have not put me on the back burner. My story matters to You, even when I can't see where it's going.

Help me trust Your timing without feeling abandoned by it.

In Jesus' name, Amen.

WEDNESDAY PRAYER

Lord, I need to hear from You.

Not in a dramatic way. Not through signs or miracles. I just need to feel Your presence. To know that You're still with me. That I haven't been left to figure this out on my own.

Sometimes Your silence feels heavier than I can carry. I pray and hear nothing. I wait and see no movement. And I start to wonder if You're even listening.

Remind me that Your presence isn't dependent on my ability to feel it. That You're here whether I sense You or not. That Your love for me doesn't rise and fall with my emotions.

Speak to my heart today. Even if it's just a whisper. I'm listening.

In Jesus' name, Amen.

THURSDAY PRAYER

God, help me stop comparing my story to everyone else's.

It's killing me. Every engagement announcement feels like evidence that I'm falling behind. Every "save the date" feels like confirmation that everyone else is chosen and I'm not.

I know comparison is poison, but I don't know how to stop drinking it.

Teach me to celebrate with others without diminishing my own journey. Teach me to trust that my timeline doesn't have to match anyone else's. Teach me that being single right now doesn't mean being forgotten.

You have a story for my life. It doesn't look like theirs, and that's okay. Help me stop measuring my worth by someone else's chapters.

In Jesus' name, Amen.

FRIDAY PRAYER

Father, I'm holding onto Your promises.

You said You would never leave me or forsake me. You said You know the plans You have for me. You said You work all things together for the good of those who love You.

I'm choosing to believe those promises today, even when my circumstances don't reflect them yet.

You have not forgotten me. You have not abandoned my story. You are working, even when I can't see it.

Anchor me in that truth. When doubt creeps in, when fear whispers lies, when loneliness threatens to swallow me whole, remind me that You are faithful. Always.

I am not forgotten. I am not overlooked. I am Yours.

In Jesus' name, Amen.

SATURDAY PRAYER

God, thank You for seeing me.

Not just knowing about me, but actually seeing me. Seeing the ache I don't talk about. Seeing the hope I'm afraid to admit. Seeing the fear that maybe I'll be alone forever.

You see all of it. And You haven't turned away.

This week, You reminded me that I'm not forgotten. That my story matters. That You're present, even when I can't feel You.

Help me carry that truth into the week ahead. When the lies come back, and they will, help me remember this moment. This prayer. This promise.

I am seen. I am known. I am not forgotten.

In Jesus' name, Amen.

SUNDAY REFLECTION

Reflect:

- When do you most feel forgotten? What triggers that feeling?

- What would change in your life if you truly believed God sees you, right now, exactly as you are?

Declare:

- I am not forgotten.

- God sees me completely and loves me fully.

- My story matters to Him.

> Carry This: "Can a mother forget the baby at her breast and have no compassion on the child she has borne? Though she may forget, I will not forget you! See, I have engraved you on the palms of my hands.", Isaiah 49:15-16a (NIV)

SUNDAY PRAYER

God, You reminded me this week that I'm not forgotten.

When everything around me screamed otherwise, when my circumstances looked like abandonment, You spoke truth. You see me. You know me. You haven't overlooked my story.

Help me carry that truth into the week ahead. When the lies come back, when I start to doubt again, bring me back to this moment. Remind me that I am seen.

In Jesus' name, Amen.

WEEK 3: YOU ARE NOT UNFINISHED

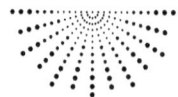

MONDAY DEVOTIONAL

You are not a half waiting for a whole.

Let that sink in for a moment, because it goes against everything our culture teaches. Movies, songs, social media, even well-meaning people in the church, everyone pushes the narrative that you're incomplete until someone completes you.

"You complete me."

"My better half."

"My other half."

It sounds romantic. It sounds poetic. But it's a lie that's doing real damage to how you see yourself.

Here's the truth Scripture actually teaches: You were made complete in Christ. Not in a relationship. Not in marriage. Not when someone finally chooses you.

In Colossians 2:10, Paul writes:

> "...and in Christ you have been brought to fullness" (NIV).

Fullness. Not partial. Not lacking. Not waiting for another human to make you whole.

Fullness.

The Enemy loves the "incomplete" narrative because it makes you vulnerable. If you believe you're only half a person, you'll settle for anyone who makes you feel whole, even temporarily. You'll compromise boundaries. You'll ignore red flags. You'll hand over pieces of yourself to people who were never meant to carry them.

All because you believed the lie that you're unfinished.

But you're not.

Yes, you're still growing. Yes, you're still healing. Yes, there are areas of your life that need work. That's called being human. That's called sanctification. That's the process God walks every single person through, married or single.

But growth is not the same as incompleteness.

You are not a rough draft waiting for someone to edit you into the final version. You are not a half-written story waiting for another character to make you interesting. You are not a puzzle missing a piece.

You are whole in Christ. Right now. Today.

That doesn't mean you don't desire companionship, that's a God-given desire. It doesn't mean you wouldn't thrive in a healthy relationship, many people do. It doesn't mean you're not allowed to want partnership.

It means your worth, your identity, and your completeness are not on hold until someone shows up.

You are not unfinished.

You are whole.

And the sooner you believe that, the freer you'll be.

MONDAY PRAYER

God, I've believed the lie that I'm incomplete.

I've looked at my life and thought, "Something's missing." I've looked at couples and thought, "They have what I don't." I've treated singleness like being half a person instead of being whole in You.

Forgive me for allowing the world's definitions to override Yours. Forgive me for believing I need someone else to validate my worth. Forgive me for thinking I'm unfinished when You've already made me complete in Christ.

Teach me what it means to be whole, not because I have it all together, but because I have You.

I don't want to spend another day believing I'm less than I am. Help me see myself the way You see me: fully loved, fully seen, fully complete.

In Jesus' name, Amen.

TUESDAY PRAYER

Father, I'm tired of waiting to feel complete.

I've put so much of my identity on hold, thinking, "When I meet someone, then I'll be whole. Then my life will really start. Then I'll finally be enough."

But that's not what You say about me.

You say I'm complete in Christ. You say I lack nothing because I have You. You say my identity isn't found in another person, it's found in You alone.

Help me stop living like I'm in a holding pattern. Help me stop treating today like it doesn't count because I'm single. Help me embrace this season as part of my story, not a gap before the real story begins.

I am whole. Today. Right now. Because of You.

In Jesus' name, Amen.

WEDNESDAY PRAYER

Lord, I don't want to bring brokenness into a relationship.

I know I need to be whole before I can be healthy with someone else. But I'm afraid that "becoming whole" means I have to be perfect first. That I have to have everything figured out. That I can't desire relationship until I'm completely healed.

And that feels impossible.

Show me the difference between wholeness and perfection. Remind me that being whole doesn't mean being flawless, it means being rooted in You. It means my identity is secure. It means I'm not looking for someone else to fix me.

I don't have to be perfect to be ready. But I do need to be whole. And that only happens in You.

In Jesus' name, Amen.

THURSDAY PRAYER

God, help me stop searching for completion in people.

I've done it before. I've looked to relationships to fill voids only You can fill. I've expected people to meet needs they were never designed to meet. And when they couldn't, I thought something was wrong with them, or worse, with me.

But the problem wasn't them. It was that I was asking them to be my source when You're the only true source I need.

Teach me to find my completeness in You first. Teach me to be so rooted in Your love that I don't need anyone else to validate me. Teach me what it means to desire companionship without demanding it complete me.

I want to be whole before I invite anyone into my life. And wholeness only comes from You.

In Jesus' name, Amen.

FRIDAY PRAYER

Father, I'm letting go of the "better half" lie.

I am not half a person. I am not incomplete. I am not waiting for someone to finish what You've already started in me.

I am whole because of Christ. I am complete because of Your love. I am enough because You say I am.

If You bring someone into my life, it won't be to complete me, it will be to walk alongside someone who is already complete in You. Two whole people, building something together.

But until then, I refuse to live like I'm unfinished. I refuse to treat singleness like a deficiency. I refuse to believe the lie that I'm less than I am.

I am whole. And that's the truth I'm standing on.

In Jesus' name, Amen.

SATURDAY PRAYER

God, thank You for making me complete.

Not through a relationship. Not through achievement. Not through anyone or anything except Christ.

This week, You've been rewriting the lies I believed about myself. You've been replacing "unfinished" with "whole." You've been reminding me that my identity is secure, not because of who's beside me, but because of who lives in me.

Help me walk in that truth. When the world tries to convince me I'm lacking, remind me of this week. Remind me that I am complete, whole, and fully loved, right now.

In Jesus' name, Amen.

SUNDAY REFLECTION

Reflect:

- Where have you believed the lie that you're "incomplete" without someone?

- What would change if you truly believed you're whole in Christ today?

Declare:

- I am not unfinished.

- I am complete in Christ.

- My worth is not determined by my relationship status.

CARRY THIS: "...and in Christ you have been brought to fullness. He is the head over every power and authority.", Colossians 2:10 (NIV)

SUNDAY PRAYER

God, I've believed the lie that I'm incomplete for so long.

This week, You started rewriting that narrative. You reminded me that I'm whole in You, not in another person. That completeness is already mine.

Help me live from that truth. When the world tries to convince me otherwise, anchor me in what You say. I am complete. Today.
Right now.

In Jesus' name, Amen.

WEEK 4: YOUR SINGLENESS IS NOT PUNISHMENT

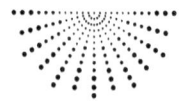

MONDAY DEVOTIONAL

Let's address the thought you've been afraid to say out loud: "What did I do wrong?"

Maybe you've wondered if God is withholding a relationship because you messed up somewhere. Maybe you've replayed past relationships, trying to figure out which mistake cost you your future. Maybe you've looked at your life and thought, "If I were more obedient, more faithful, more... something... He would bless me with what I'm asking for."

Maybe you've started to believe that your singleness is punishment.

It's not.

Let me say that again, because the Enemy has been whispering lies long enough:

Your singleness is not punishment.

It's not penance for past mistakes. It's not God withholding good things because you're not good enough. It's not evidence that you've failed some spiritual test.

God doesn't operate like that.

In John 9, the disciples encounter a man who was born blind. They immediately ask Jesus,

> "Rabbi, who sinned, this man or his parents, that he was born blind?" (John 9:2, NIV).

They assumed suffering equaled punishment. Hardship equaled sin. Difficulty equaled divine discipline.

Jesus' response cuts through that lie:

> "Neither this man nor his parents sinned," said Jesus, "but this happened so that the works of God might be displayed in him" (John 9:3, NIV).

Not everything hard in your life is punishment. Not every unanswered prayer is evidence of wrongdoing. Not every delay is discipline.

Sometimes, God is working something in you that you can't see yet.

Now, let's be honest: maybe you have made mistakes. Maybe there are patterns in your past relationships that need healing. Maybe there are areas where you need to grow before you're ready for what you're asking for.

That's not punishment, that's preparation.

God loves you too much to give you something you're not ready to steward well. He loves you too much to rush you into a relationship that would harm you. He loves you too much to ignore the healing you need just to meet your timeline.

But hear this clearly: singleness is not a consequence. It's a season.

And seasons serve a purpose.

You are not being punished. You are not being overlooked. You are not paying for past failures.

You are being loved, even when it doesn't feel like it. You are being shaped, even when it's uncomfortable. You are being prepared, even when you don't understand why.

God is not withholding good from you out of anger.

He's withholding less than His best because He loves you too much to settle.

MONDAY PRAYER

God, I've believed You were punishing me.

I've looked at my singleness and thought, "This must be my fault." I've replayed every mistake, every failed relationship, every moment I didn't trust You enough, and I've convinced myself that this is the consequence.

But that's not who You are.

You don't withhold love as punishment. You don't use singleness as discipline. You don't keep good things from me because I haven't earned them.

Forgive me for believing lies about Your character. Forgive me for thinking my worth is tied to my performance. Forgive me for treating this season like a sentence instead of a gift.

Help me see this season through Your eyes, not as punishment, but as preparation. Not as rejection, but as redirection. Not as withholding, but as waiting for the right time.

I am not being punished. I am being loved.

In Jesus' name, Amen.

TUESDAY PRAYER

Father, I need to stop blaming myself.

I've carried so much guilt about being single, like it's proof I've done something wrong. I've looked at my past and thought, "If I had made different choices, maybe I'd be married by now."

But I can't change the past. And honestly, I don't know if my choices are even the reason I'm here.

What I do know is this: You don't operate on shame. You don't lead through guilt. You don't punish me for being human.

Help me release the weight I've been carrying. Help me stop torturing myself with "what ifs" and "if onlys." Help me trust that You're not holding my past against me.

You've already forgiven me. Help me forgive myself.

In Jesus' name, Amen.

WEDNESDAY PRAYER

Lord, I've confused delay with denial.

When You don't answer my prayers on my timeline, I assume the answer is no. When circumstances don't change quickly, I assume I've done something wrong. When relationships don't work out, I assume You're punishing me.

But delay doesn't mean denial. Waiting doesn't mean withholding. Closed doors don't mean You're angry with me.

Teach me to trust Your timing without questioning Your love. Teach me that sometimes the best gift is the one that comes later, when I'm truly ready for it. Teach me that Your "not yet" is not the same as "never."

You're not punishing me with waiting. You're protecting me in it.

In Jesus' name, Amen.

THURSDAY PRAYER

God, I don't want to carry this fear anymore.

The fear that I've disqualified myself. The fear that I've messed up too much. The fear that even if You wanted to bless me, I've burned through my chances.

That's not how Your grace works. That's not how Your love operates. That's not who You are.

You don't have a quota on second chances. You don't run out of mercy. You don't look at my life and think, "Too late. Too broken. Too far gone."

You look at me and see someone worth redeeming. Someone worth restoring. Someone worth loving, no matter how many times I've stumbled.

Help me believe that. Help me stop living in fear of punishment and start living in the freedom of Your grace.

In Jesus' name, Amen.

FRIDAY PRAYER

Father, help me see this season differently.

Not as punishment, but as preparation. Not as abandonment, but as intention. Not as proof that I'm failing, but as evidence that You're working.

I don't know what You're preparing me for. I don't know how long this season will last. I don't know what the purpose is yet.

But I'm choosing to trust that You're not wasting this time. That every moment of waiting has meaning. That You're shaping me into someone who can handle what's coming next.

This is not punishment. This is process. And I'm trusting You with it.

In Jesus' name, Amen.

SATURDAY PRAYER

God, thank You for loving me, not punishing me.

Thank You for being patient with my doubts. Thank You for not giving up on me when I've questioned Your goodness. Thank You for continuing to work in me, even when I've misunderstood Your motives.

This week, You've reminded me that singleness is not punishment, it's a season with purpose. You've reminded me that delays are not denials. You've reminded me that You love me too much to give me less than Your best.

Help me hold onto that truth when the lies come back. Help me remember who You really are.

In Jesus' name, Amen.

SUNDAY REFLECTION

Reflect:

- Have you been treating your singleness as punishment? What would it look like to see it as preparation instead?

- What lies have you believed about why you're still single?

Declare:

- My singleness is not punishment.

- God is not withholding good from me.

- This season has purpose, even when I don't understand it.

> Carry This: "For I know the plans I have for you," declares the Lord, "plans to prosper you and not to harm you, plans to give you hope and a future.", Jeremiah 29:11 (NIV)

SUNDAY PRAYER

God, I've carried so much shame about being single.

I've believed it was proof I did something wrong, that You were withholding good from me as discipline. But this week, You showed me that's not who You are.

You're not punishing me. You're loving me. You're preparing me. You're working something I can't see yet.

Help me trust that. Help me stop questioning Your heart toward me.

In Jesus' name, Amen.

WEEK 5: THIS IS NOT A WAITING ROOM

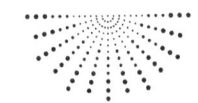

MONDAY DEVOTIONAL

You need to stop putting your life on pause.

I know that sounds harsh, but it's true. And if no one else is going to say it to you, I will:

Your life is happening right now. Not when you meet someone. Not when you get married. Not when your circumstances finally look the way you want them to.

Right now.

And if you spend this entire season waiting for the "real" part of your life to begin, you're going to wake up one day, whether that's in a relationship or still single, and realize you missed it.

You missed the friendships you could have deepened because you were too focused on finding "the one." You missed the dreams you could have pursued because you thought, "I'll do that when I'm settled." You missed the growth, the joy, the purpose, the calling, all of it, because you convinced yourself this season didn't count.

But it does count.

Every day you're single counts. Every moment you're waiting counts. Every season that doesn't look like what you planned, it all counts.

This is not a waiting room. This is your life.

In Luke 19, Jesus tells a parable about a master who gives his servants money and tells them,

> **"Put this money to work... until I come back" (Luke 19:13, NIV).**

He didn't say, "Sit here and wait for me to return."

He said, "Put this to work."

That's what God is saying to you today. You have this season, however long it lasts. You have these days, these months, maybe these years. And He's not asking you to sit in a holding pattern until something changes.

He's asking you to live fully in the season you're in.

Does that mean you stop hoping for a relationship? No.

Does that mean you stop praying for a partner? Absolutely not.

But it does mean you stop treating today like it doesn't matter. It means you stop saying, "I'll start that business when I'm married." "I'll travel when I have someone to go with." "I'll pursue that dream when my life is more settled."

Your life is settled right now. Maybe not in the way you wanted. Maybe not in the way you planned. But it's settled enough to start living.

Stop waiting for permission to thrive. Stop waiting for someone to validate your choices. Stop waiting for your circumstances to be perfect before you start building the life God has called you to.

This is not a waiting room.

This is your life.

And it's time to start living it.

MONDAY PRAYER

God, I've been living in a holding pattern.

I've treated this season like it's temporary, like it doesn't really count until something changes. I've put dreams on hold, relationships on pause, and parts of myself in storage, waiting for the "right time" to pull them back out.

But the right time is now.

Forgive me for wasting the season You've given me. Forgive me for treating singleness like a waiting room instead of a season with purpose. Forgive me for believing the lie that my life doesn't really start until someone shows up.

Teach me to live fully right now. Teach me to invest in this season instead of wishing it away. Teach me that waiting for Your timing doesn't mean putting my entire life on pause.

Help me stop waiting and start living.

In Jesus' name, Amen.

TUESDAY PRAYER

Father, I don't want to waste this season.

I look back at the last year, or the last several years, and I'm afraid I've missed it. I've been so focused on what I don't have that I haven't fully lived in what I do have.

But I don't want to do that anymore.

I want to be present. I want to pursue the dreams You've placed in my heart. I want to build friendships, serve in Your kingdom, grow in my calling, all of it. I don't want to wait until I'm married to start living the life You've called me to.

Give me courage to take the first step. Give me clarity about what You're calling me to do in this season. Give me the boldness to stop making excuses and start moving forward.

This season matters. And I'm choosing to live like it does.

In Jesus' name, Amen.

WEDNESDAY PRAYER

Lord, I've been using singleness as an excuse.

An excuse not to take risks. An excuse not to pursue dreams. An excuse to stay comfortable and avoid the hard work of growth.

I've told myself, "When I'm married, then I'll have the stability to do that." But the truth is, I'm afraid. And it's easier to blame my singleness than to face my fear.

But You haven't given me a spirit of fear. You've given me power, love, and a sound mind.

Help me stop hiding behind "when I'm married" and start stepping into what You've called me to do today. Help me stop waiting for someone else to give me permission to live fully. Help me be brave enough to pursue purpose right now.

This season is not an excuse. It's an opportunity.

In Jesus' name, Amen.

THURSDAY PRAYER

God, teach me to steward this season well.

I know that how I live today matters. I know that the choices I make now, whether I grow or coast, whether I invest or withdraw, whether I thrive or survive, will shape who I become.

I don't want to look back on this time with regret. I don't want to realize I spent years waiting instead of living. I don't want to waste the gifts, the opportunities, the moments You've given me.

Show me what it looks like to steward singleness well. Show me how to be faithful with what I have today, even while I hope for something different tomorrow. Show me how to live fully without demanding my circumstances change first.

This season is a gift. Help me treat it like one.

In Jesus' name, Amen.

FRIDAY PRAYER

Father, I release my timeline.

I've been holding onto it so tightly, trying to control when things happen, trying to force doors open, trying to make my life look a certain way by a certain age.

But that's not trust. That's control.

And I'm tired of fighting You for control of my story.

So I'm releasing it. My timeline. My expectations. My demands that You work on my schedule.

I'm choosing to trust that Your timing is better than mine. That Your plans are bigger than mine. That even when I can't see what You're doing, You're working for my good.

Teach me to live fully in the season I'm in, without demanding to know when it will end.

In Jesus' name, Amen.

SATURDAY PRAYER

God, thank You for the gift of today.

Thank You for reminding me that this is not a waiting room, it's my life. Thank You for calling me to live fully, right now, in the season You've given me.

This week, You've challenged me to stop coasting and start investing. To stop waiting and start living. To stop treating singleness like a problem and start seeing it as an opportunity.

Help me carry that truth forward. When I'm tempted to put life on hold again, remind me of this week. Remind me that every day matters. Every season counts. And You've given me this time for a reason.

In Jesus' name, Amen.

SUNDAY REFLECTION

Reflect:

- What have you put on hold, waiting for your circumstances to change?

- What would it look like to fully live in this season, right now?

Declare:

- This is not a waiting room. This is my life.

- I will not waste this season.

- I am choosing to live fully, right now.

> **Carry This: "This is the day the Lord has made; let us rejoice and be glad in it.", Psalm 118:24 (NIV)**

SUNDAY PRAYER

God, I've been putting my life on hold.

Waiting for the "right time" to pursue dreams, to invest in relationships, to actually live. But this week, You challenged me to stop waiting and start living.

Give me courage to move forward. To pursue what You've placed on my heart. To stop treating this season like it doesn't count.

My life is happening right now. Help me live it.

In Jesus' name, Amen.

WEEK 6: FULLY LOVED, FULLY SEEN, FULLY ENOUGH

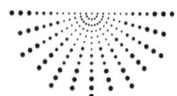

MONDAY DEVOTIONAL

You've spent so much time trying to become enough.

Enough to be noticed. Enough to be chosen. Enough to be loved.

You've worked on yourself, your appearance, your personality, your career, your spirituality, thinking that if you could just fix the right things, improve the right areas, become the right version of yourself, then finally, someone would see you and think, "Yes. You're enough."

But here's what you need to understand:

You already are.

Not because you've perfected yourself. Not because you've checked all the boxes. Not because you've earned it.

But because God says so.

And His voice is the only one that actually matters.

The world will always tell you you're not enough. You're not thin enough, successful enough, interesting enough, spiritual enough, put-together enough. There will always be another standard to meet, another comparison to lose, another way you fall short.

But God doesn't measure you that way.

In Romans 5:8, Paul writes something that should fundamentally reshape how you see yourself:

> **"But God demonstrates his own love for us in this: While we were still sinners, Christ died for us" (NIV).**

While we were still sinners.

Not after we cleaned ourselves up. Not when we finally got it right. Not when we became worthy.

While we were still broken, still messy, still struggling, He loved us. Completely. Fully. Enough to die for us.

If God loved you when you were at your worst, why do you think you have to be at your best to be loved now?

You don't.

You are fully loved, not because of what you bring to the table, but because of who sits at the head of it.

You are fully seen, not just the parts you show the world, but the parts you hide. The insecurities. The wounds. The fears. He sees all of it, and He doesn't flinch.

You are fully enough, not because you've achieved some standard of perfection, but because His love isn't conditional.

Now, does that mean you stop growing? No.

Does that mean you stop working on yourself? Absolutely not.

But it does mean you stop tying your worth to your progress. It means you stop believing the lie that you have to earn love. It means you stop living like you're one improvement away from being acceptable.

You are loved. You are seen. You are enough.

Right now. Today. Exactly as you are.

Believe that, and everything changes.

MONDAY PRAYER

God, I've been trying to earn what You've already given me.

I've been working so hard to become "enough", enough to be loved, enough to be chosen, enough to be seen. I've believed the lie that if I could just fix myself, improve myself, perfect myself, then finally I'd be worthy.

But that's not how Your love works.

You loved me before I did anything to deserve it. You saw me when I was at my worst and chose me anyway. You called me enough before I believed it myself.

Forgive me for doubting Your love. Forgive me for treating it like something I have to earn instead of something You've freely given. Forgive me for believing I'm only as valuable as my latest achievement.

Teach me to rest in Your love. Teach me that I don't have to perform for Your approval. Teach me that I am fully loved, fully seen, fully enough, not because of who I am, but because of who You are.

In Jesus' name, Amen.

TUESDAY PRAYER

Father, I need You to silence the voices that say I'm not enough.

The voice of comparison that says everyone else has it together except me. The voice of perfectionism that says I have to be flawless to be lovable. The voice of rejection that replays every time I wasn't chosen and convinces me I never will be.

Those voices are loud. And on my worst days, I believe them.

But they're not Your voice.

Your voice says I'm loved. Your voice says I'm seen. Your voice says I'm enough, not because I've earned it, but because You've declared it.

Help me hear You above the noise. Help me silence the lies with Your truth. Help me believe what You say about me more than what the world says, what my past says, or what my insecurities say.

I am enough because You say I am. And that's the only voice that matters.

In Jesus' name, Amen.

WEDNESDAY PRAYER

Lord, I don't know how to stop striving.

I've spent so long trying to be enough that I don't know how to just... be. I don't know how to rest in Your love without feeling like I need to do something to keep it. I don't know how to believe I'm fully seen without trying to manage what You see.

But striving isn't the same as trusting. And performing isn't the same as being loved.

Teach me to rest. Teach me that Your love isn't something I maintain through effort, it's something You sustain through grace. Teach me that I don't have to hustle for worth I already have.

I am loved. Not because I'm perfect, but because You are. And that's enough.

In Jesus' name, Amen.

THURSDAY PRAYER

God, I've been measuring my worth by whether someone chooses me.

Every time a relationship doesn't work out, I take it as evidence that I'm not enough. Every time I'm overlooked, I assume it's because I'm lacking something. Every time someone else gets chosen and I don't, I spiral into "what's wrong with me?"

But my worth isn't determined by who picks me. It's determined by who already has, You.

You chose me before I was born. You called me by name. You loved me enough to die for me. And nothing, no rejection, no breakup, no person who walks away, can change that.

Help me stop handing my worth over to people who were never meant to define it. Help me anchor my identity in You, not in whether someone sees my value. Help me believe that I am fully loved, fully seen, fully enough, whether anyone else notices or not.

In Jesus' name, Amen.

FRIDAY PRAYER

Father, I want to live from a place of "enough," not toward it.

I don't want to spend the rest of my life chasing worth, trying to prove I'm valuable, hustling to be seen. I don't want to base my identity on what I achieve, who I attract, or how I measure up.

I want to live from the truth that I'm already enough. That Your love has already settled the question. That I don't have to earn what You've already given.

Teach me what that looks like. Teach me how to stop striving and start resting. Teach me how to walk in the fullness of who You say I am, instead of the scarcity of who the world says I should be.

I am loved. I am seen. I am enough. Today and every day.

In Jesus' name, Amen.

SATURDAY PRAYER

God, thank You for loving me as I am.

Not as I should be. Not as I will be. But as I am, right now, in this moment.

Thank You for seeing all of me, the good, the broken, the messy, the beautiful, and not turning away.

Thank You for declaring me enough, even when I don't feel like it. Thank You for choosing me, even when others haven't. Thank You for never requiring me to earn what You've already freely given.

This week, You've reminded me that I am fully loved, fully seen, fully enough. Help me live in that truth. Help me stop performing for approval I already have.

In Jesus' name, Amen.

SUNDAY REFLECTION

Reflect:

- Where have you been trying to "earn" love instead of receiving it?

- What would change if you truly believed you were fully loved, fully seen, and fully enough, right now?

Declare:

- I am fully loved by God.

- I am fully seen by God.

- I am fully enough because God says I am.

> Carry This: "See what great love the Father has lavished on us, that we should be called children of God! And that is what we are!" , 1 John 3:1a (NIV)

SUNDAY PRAYER

God, I've been hustling for worth I already have.

Trying to earn love, prove my value, become "enough" for someone to choose me. But this week, You reminded me that I already am. In You.

Help me rest in that. Help me stop performing and start receiving. Help me believe that I'm fully loved, fully seen, fully enough, right now.

In Jesus' name, Amen.

WEEK 7: WHEN EVERYONE ELSE'S STORY FEELS BETTER THAN YOURS

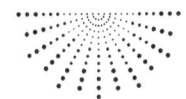

MONDAY DEVOTIONAL

Comparison will destroy you faster than almost anything else.

It's subtle. It doesn't announce itself. It just creeps in when you're scrolling through social media, sitting in church, talking to a friend who just got engaged, and suddenly, you're measuring your life against theirs.

And losing.

Their relationship looks easier. Their timeline looks faster. Their story looks... better.

And yours? Yours feels stuck. Slow. Like you're falling further behind every day.

Here's the truth you need to hear:

You're not falling behind. You're on a completely different path.

Comparison doesn't work because it assumes everyone is running the same race toward the same finish line. But that's not how God works. He's not handing out identical lives and grading you based on who gets there first.

He's writing individual stories. Unique callings. Different timelines.

And the moment you start measuring your Chapter 3 against someone else's Chapter 10, you lose sight of what God is actually doing in your life.

In 2 Corinthians 10:12, Paul writes:

> **"We do not dare to classify or compare ourselves with some who commend themselves. When they measure themselves by themselves and compare themselves with themselves, they are not wise" (NIV).**

They are not wise.

Comparison isn't just painful, it's foolish. Because it's asking the wrong question.

The question isn't, "Why does their story look better than mine?"

The question is, "What is God doing in my story that I'm missing because I'm too busy watching theirs?"

Maybe God is using this season to heal something in you that needed time. Maybe He's building character that can only be formed through waiting. Maybe He's redirecting your path away from something that looked good but wasn't actually good for you.

You don't know what's happening behind the scenes of anyone else's life. You don't know what they're walking through, what they've sacrificed, what struggles they're hiding behind the highlight reel.

And honestly? It doesn't matter.

Because their story isn't yours. And trying to live their timeline will only rob you of the beauty in your own.

God has not forgotten about you. He has not given everyone else the better story. He has not ranked you last.

He's just writing something different. And different doesn't mean less.

Stop comparing. Stop measuring. Stop ranking.

Your story matters. Exactly as it is.

MONDAY PRAYER

God, comparison is eating me alive.

I can't stop looking at other people's lives and feeling like I'm losing. Every engagement announcement feels like proof I'm falling behind. Every couple I see feels like evidence that everyone else is getting what I'm not.

And I hate it. I hate feeling this way. I hate that I can't just be happy for people without feeling sad for myself. I hate that I've turned my life into a competition I can never win.

Forgive me. Forgive me for measuring my worth by someone else's timeline. Forgive me for treating Your blessings like a ranking system. Forgive me for doubting Your goodness just because my story doesn't look like theirs.

Teach me to stop comparing. Teach me to celebrate others without diminishing myself. Teach me that my story matters, even when it looks nothing like the stories around me.

Help me fix my eyes on You, not on them.

In Jesus' name, Amen.

TUESDAY PRAYER

Father, I need You to heal the jealousy in my heart.

I don't want to feel this way. I don't want to resent people for finding love. I don't want to scroll past engagement photos with bitterness instead of joy. But I do. And I'm ashamed of it.

I know jealousy is a poison. I know it's destroying my peace, my relationships, my ability to see Your goodness in my own life. But I don't know how to stop feeling it.

So I'm asking You to do what I can't. Heal this wound. Remove the bitterness. Replace jealousy with genuine joy. Help me celebrate what You're doing in other people's lives without feeling robbed of what You're doing in mine.

I don't want comparison to steal my joy anymore.

In Jesus' name, Amen.

WEDNESDAY PRAYER

Lord, help me stop scrolling and start living.

Social media is killing me. Every time I open it, I'm bombarded with proof that everyone else is moving forward and I'm not. Engagements. Weddings. Babies. Picture-perfect lives that make mine feel small and insignificant.

I know it's not the full story. I know everyone's posting highlights, not reality. But knowing that doesn't stop it from hurting.

Give me the strength to step back. To stop feeding the comparison monster. To protect my heart from the constant noise that says I'm not enough, I'm not where I should be, I'm falling behind.

Teach me to focus on my own race, not everyone else's. Teach me to measure my life by Your truth, not their posts.

In Jesus' name, Amen.

THURSDAY PRAYER

God, remind me that different doesn't mean less.

My story doesn't look like anyone else's. My timeline doesn't match theirs. My journey is slower, harder, more complicated than I thought it would be.

But that doesn't mean it's worse.

You're not comparing me to anyone else. You're not ranking my progress. You're not disappointed that my life doesn't look like theirs.

You're writing a story that's uniquely mine. And it's exactly what I need, even when I don't understand it.

Help me believe that. Help me stop wishing I had someone else's story and start embracing the one You've given me. Help me trust that You're doing something good, even when it looks different from what I expected.

Different doesn't mean less. It just means different.

In Jesus' name, Amen.

FRIDAY PRAYER

Father, teach me contentment in my own story.

Not contentment that stops hoping. Not contentment that stops praying. But contentment that lets me live fully in the season I'm in, without constantly wishing I was in someone else's.

I want to be able to celebrate with others without feeling less-than. I want to be able to see their joy without it triggering my pain. I want to be genuinely happy for them, because I'm genuinely confident in what You're doing in me.

Give me that kind of peace. The kind that doesn't depend on my circumstances matching everyone else's. The kind that trusts You're working, even when the results look different.

I am not behind. I am exactly where You want me to be.

In Jesus' name, Amen.

SATURDAY PRAYER

God, thank You for writing my story.

Not someone else's. Not the one I thought I'd have. But the one You're writing, perfectly crafted, perfectly timed, perfectly mine.

This week, You've reminded me that comparison steals joy. That measuring my life against others robs me of the beauty in my own journey. That my story matters, even when it's different.

Help me keep my eyes on You. When I'm tempted to compare again, and I will be, remind me of this week. Remind me that You're not grading me based on someone else's timeline.

My story is mine. And it's exactly what I need.

In Jesus' name, Amen.

SUNDAY REFLECTION

Reflect:

- Who do you compare yourself to most often? What about their story triggers your insecurity?

- What beauty in your own story are you missing because you're too busy watching theirs?

Declare:

- I am not falling behind.

- My story matters, exactly as it is.

- God is writing something uniquely mine, and I trust Him with it.

> Carry This: "But each one should test their own actions. Then they can take pride in themselves alone, without comparing themselves to someone else.", Galatians 6:4 (NIV)

SUNDAY PRAYER

God, comparison has been poisoning me.

Making me bitter, jealous, resentful. This week, You showed me that my story matters, even when it looks nothing like anyone else's.

Help me keep my eyes on You instead of on them. Help me celebrate without comparing. Help me trust that You're writing something good in my life, even when it's different.

In Jesus' name, Amen.

WEEK 8: GOD'S DESIGN FOR THIS SEASON

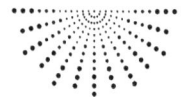

MONDAY DEVOTIONAL

What if this season isn't a mistake?

What if it's not something you have to endure, survive, or push through as quickly as possible?

What if God actually designed it, intentionally, purposefully, specifically for you?

That's a hard thought to sit with, especially when this season feels more like punishment than purpose. But what if it's true?

What if singleness isn't God's Plan B? What if it's not the result of bad timing, bad choices, or being overlooked? What if it's exactly where He wants you, for reasons you can't see yet?

In 1 Corinthians 7, Paul writes something most Christians skip over because it's uncomfortable:

> "I wish that all of you were as I am. But each of you has your own gift from God; one has this gift, another has that" (1 Corinthians 7:7, NIV).

Paul calls singleness a gift.

Not a curse. Not a consolation prize. Not something to tolerate until the "real" gift shows up.

A gift.

Now, that doesn't mean singleness feels like a gift right now. It doesn't mean you have to love every moment of it or pretend it's easy. It doesn't mean you're not allowed to desire marriage.

But it does mean this: God has a purpose for this season that goes beyond just waiting for the next one.

Maybe He's using this time to heal wounds that a relationship would have only complicated. Maybe He's developing character in you that will serve you for the rest of your life. Maybe He's redirecting your path away from something that looked good but would have derailed you.

Maybe He's teaching you to find your identity in Him instead of in another person. Maybe He's showing you what it means to be complete before you're coupled. Maybe He's preparing you for something bigger than you've even imagined yet.

Or maybe, and this is the hardest one to accept, maybe He's calling you to a season (or a lifetime) of singleness because He has something for you to do that requires your undivided devotion.

You won't know which one it is until you stop resenting the season and start asking, "God, what are You doing here? What are You trying to show me? What are You building in me that I wouldn't learn any other way?"

This season has purpose.

Not because it's easy. Not because it's fun. Not because it's what you would have chosen.

But because God designed it. And He doesn't waste anything.

MONDAY PRAYER

God, I've been treating this season like a mistake.

Like something went wrong. Like You forgot about me or messed up the timeline. Like singleness is proof that I'm off-track instead of exactly where You want me.

But what if I'm wrong? What if this season isn't a mistake, it's intentional? What if You actually designed it for a reason I can't see yet?

Forgive me for resenting what You've allowed. Forgive me for treating this season like something to survive instead of something to steward. Forgive me for assuming You're withholding good from me instead of trusting that You're working something in me.

Help me see this season through Your eyes. Show me the purpose I've been missing. Teach me what You're building in me that I couldn't learn any other way.

This season has meaning. Help me find it.

In Jesus' name, Amen.

TUESDAY PRAYER

Father, I don't understand why I'm here.

I don't understand why my life looks like this. I don't understand why You've kept me single when I've been ready, so ready, for something more. I don't understand what You're waiting for, what You're doing, or how long this will last.

But I'm choosing to trust You anyway.

Not because I have answers. Not because this feels good. But because I believe You're not wasting this time. I believe You have a purpose for this season, even when I can't see it. I believe You're working something in me that matters.

Help me stop demanding explanations and start trusting Your design. Help me believe that even when I don't understand, You do. And that's enough.

In Jesus' name, Amen.

WEDNESDAY PRAYER

Lord, what are You trying to teach me?

I don't want to waste this season. I don't want to spend years resenting it, only to realize later that I missed what You were trying to show me.

So I'm asking: What are You trying to teach me? What are You building in me? What are You healing, shaping, refining during this time?

Open my eyes to see it. Open my heart to receive it. Help me stop fighting this season and start learning from it.

If there's purpose here, I want to find it. If there's growth available, I want to embrace it. If You're doing something in me that I can't do anywhere else, I don't want to miss it.

Teach me, Lord. I'm listening.

In Jesus' name, Amen.

THURSDAY PRAYER

God, help me stop resenting Your design.

I've spent so much time angry at this season. Angry at You for allowing it. Angry at myself for being here. Angry at everyone else for moving forward while I'm stuck.

But resentment is poisoning me. It's keeping me from seeing what You're doing. It's blinding me to the purpose You've placed in this season.

I don't want to be bitter anymore. I don't want to spend the rest of this time fighting You. I want to surrender to Your design, even when I don't understand it.

Help me trust that You know what You're doing. That Your plans for me are good, even when they don't match mine. That this season, however long it lasts, is not wasted time.

In Jesus' name, Amen.

FRIDAY PRAYER

Father, I release my timeline and surrender to Yours.

I've been holding onto my plans so tightly. I've been demanding that You work on my schedule, in my way, according to my expectations. And when You didn't, I assumed You weren't listening.

But You were. You just had a different design.

So I'm releasing my grip. I'm letting go of my timeline and trusting Yours. I'm choosing to believe that Your design for this season is better than anything I could have planned.

If You're keeping me single for a reason, I trust You. If You're preparing me for something I'm not ready for yet, I trust You. If You're redirecting my path, I trust You.

Your design is perfect, even when I don't understand it.

In Jesus' name, Amen.

SATURDAY PRAYER

God, thank You for intentional design.

Thank You for not leaving my life to chance. Thank You for not letting me drift aimlessly. Thank You for designing this season with purpose, even when I couldn't see it.

This week, You've challenged me to stop resenting and start trusting. To stop fighting and start surrendering. To stop assuming this is a mistake and start believing it's intentional.

Help me carry that trust forward. When I'm tempted to spiral again, remind me that You are sovereign. That You don't waste seasons. That You're building something in me that matters.

This season has purpose. And I'm choosing to believe it.

In Jesus' name, Amen.

SUNDAY REFLECTION

Reflect:

- What if God intentionally designed this season for you? How does that change the way you see it?

- What might God be trying to teach you, heal in you, or build in you during this time?

Declare:

- This season is not a mistake.

- God has designed this time with purpose.

- I am exactly where He wants me to be.

Carry This: "For we are God's handiwork, created in Christ Jesus to do good works, which God prepared in advance for us to do." , Ephesians 2:10 (NIV)

SUNDAY PRAYER

God, I've been resenting this season.

Treating it like a mistake, like something went wrong. But this week, You challenged me to see it differently. To trust that You designed it with purpose.

I don't fully understand it yet. But I'm choosing to trust You. This season has meaning. And I'm asking You to show me what it is.

In Jesus' name, Amen.

WEEK 9: YOU ARE NOT HALF A PERSON

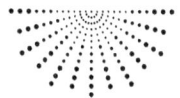

MONDAY DEVOTIONAL

The world has sold you a lie that you've probably believed your whole life:

You're incomplete without someone else.

It's everywhere. Movies, songs, books, social media, all of it reinforces the idea that you're not fully yourself until you find "the one." That you're half a person waiting for your other half. That love is what makes you whole.

And if you've believed that long enough, singleness doesn't just feel lonely, it feels like you're fundamentally lacking something.

But here's the truth:

You are not half a person.

You are a whole person, created in the image of God, with purpose, value, and identity that exists completely independent of whether someone is standing next to you.

Genesis 1:27 says:

> "So God created mankind in his own image, in the image of God he created them; male and female he created them" (NIV).

Notice what it doesn't say.

It doesn't say, "God created them incomplete, needing another person to finish them."

It doesn't say, "God created them as halves, requiring a partner to make them whole."

It says God created you, individually, uniquely, fully, in His image. You reflect God as a complete person, not as a fraction waiting for completion.

Yes, relationships are good. Yes, partnership is beautiful. Yes, marriage is a gift. But it's not a requirement for wholeness.

Adam was whole before Eve arrived. Jesus was whole and never married. Paul was whole and single. Countless people throughout history have lived full, meaningful, impactful lives without ever being in a romantic relationship.

Because wholeness doesn't come from another person.

It comes from God.

The moment you start believing you're incomplete without someone, you become vulnerable to settling for anyone who makes you feel whole, even temporarily. You overlook red flags. You compromise boundaries. You stay in relationships that hurt you because you're terrified of going back to feeling "half."

But you were never half to begin with.

You are not less than because you're single. You are not incomplete because you're unpartnered. You are not a rough draft waiting for someone to edit you into the final version.

You are fully you. Right now. Today.

And anyone who gets to walk beside you one day won't complete you, they'll complement you. Two whole people, building something together.

But until then, you are not broken. You are not lacking. You are not half.

You are whole.

MONDAY PRAYER

God, I've believed the lie that I'm incomplete.

I've looked at my life and thought, "Something's missing." I've looked at couples and thought, "They have what I don't." I've treated singleness like being half a person instead of being fully myself.

Forgive me for allowing the world's definitions to override Yours. Forgive me for believing I need someone else to make me whole. Forgive me for treating myself like a fraction when You made me complete.

Teach me what it means to be whole in You. Not because I have it all together. Not because I don't desire companionship. But because my identity, my worth, my completeness come from You alone.

I am not half a person. I am fully myself. And that's exactly who You created me to be.

In Jesus' name, Amen.

TUESDAY PRAYER

Father, I've been looking for someone to complete me.

And every time a relationship didn't work out, I felt more broken than before. Every time I was alone again, I felt like I lost a piece of myself.

But the problem wasn't them. The problem was me, looking for wholeness in a person instead of in You.

I don't want to do that anymore. I don't want to enter my next relationship from a place of lack, expecting someone to fill voids they were never meant to fill.

I want to be whole first. I want to know who I am, apart from anyone else. I want to stand secure in my identity in You before I invite someone into my life.

Teach me to stop searching for completion in people and start finding it in You.

In Jesus' name, Amen.

WEDNESDAY PRAYER

Lord, help me stop defining myself by what I don't have.

I've spent so long focusing on what's missing, a partner, a relationship, a future I can see, that I've lost sight of what I do have.

I have You. I have purpose. I have gifts, talents, passions, and a calling that matter. I have relationships, friendships, and a life that's meaningful right now, not when someone shows up, but today.

Help me shift my focus. Help me stop obsessing over what's absent and start celebrating what's present. Help me see myself as complete, not because I have everything I want, but because I have everything I need in You.

I am not defined by what I lack. I am defined by whose I am.

In Jesus' name, Amen.

THURSDAY PRAYER

God, I don't want to settle for someone just to feel whole.

I've seen it happen. I've watched people jump into relationships that hurt them because they couldn't stand being alone. I've seen them compromise, overlook red flags, and stay far longer than they should, all because they believed the lie that anything is better than being single.

I don't want to be that person.

Protect me from settling. Protect me from desperation. Protect me from believing that I need someone, anyone, to complete me.

I am already whole in You. And I'd rather be single and whole than partnered and broken.

In Jesus' name, Amen.

FRIDAY PRAYER

Father, thank You for making me complete.

Not through another person. Not through achievement. Not through anything except Christ.

You didn't create me as a fraction. You didn't design me to be half-functional until someone else showed up. You made me fully, completely, intentionally, exactly as I am.

Help me walk in that truth. Help me stop looking for validation from people and start resting in the validation I already have from You.

I am not half a person. I am whole. And that's enough.

In Jesus' name, Amen.

SATURDAY PRAYER

God, thank You for redefining wholeness for me.

This week, You've been dismantling the lie that I'm incomplete. You've been reminding me that wholeness doesn't come from another person, it comes from You.

Help me carry that truth forward. When the world tries to convince me

I'm lacking, remind me of this week. Remind me that I am complete, whole, and fully myself in You.

I am not half a person. I am fully me. And that's exactly who You created me to be.

In Jesus' name, Amen.

SUNDAY REFLECTION

Reflect:

- Where have you believed the lie that you're "half a person" without someone?

- What would change if you truly believed you're whole in Christ today?

Declare:

- I am not half a person.

- I am whole in Christ.

- My completeness does not depend on my relationship status.

> Carry This: "I have been crucified with Christ and I no longer live, but Christ lives in me. The life I now live in the body, I live by faith in the Son of God, who loved me and gave himself for me." , Galatians 2:20 (NIV)

SUNDAY PRAYER

God, I've believed I'm incomplete without someone.

This week, You dismantled that lie. You reminded me that I'm whole in You. That I'm not a fraction waiting for completion.

Help me walk in that truth. Help me stop looking for someone to complete me and start living as someone who's already whole.

In Jesus' name, Amen.

WEEK 10: BREAKING THE "INCOMPLETE" NARRATIVE

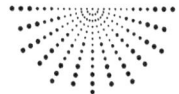

MONDAY DEVOTIONAL

There's a narrative running through your head, and it's been there so long you might not even notice it anymore:

"When I meet someone, then I'll be complete."

"When I'm in a relationship, then my life will really start."

"When I'm married, then I'll finally be whole."

It's the "incomplete" narrative. And it's been shaping your decisions, your emotions, and your sense of self-worth for longer than you realize.

Here's the problem: you can't build a healthy future on a broken foundation.

If you believe you're incomplete right now, you'll enter your next relationship from a place of desperation. You'll cling too tightly. You'll compromise too easily. You'll tolerate things you shouldn't because you're terrified of going back to feeling "less than."

And even if you do find someone, the relationship won't fix the belief.

Because the problem was never your singleness, it was the lie you believed about it.

Colossians 2:10 says:

> "...and in Christ you have been brought to fullness. He is the head over every power and authority" (NIV).

Fullness. Not partial. Not waiting. Not incomplete.

Fullness.

That's your starting point. Not your destination. Not something you achieve when circumstances align. Not something another person grants you.

You are full right now, filled with the presence of God, the love of Christ, the power of the Holy Spirit. That's what makes you complete.

Now, does that mean you stop growing? No. Does that mean you stop healing? Absolutely not. Does that mean you can't desire partnership? Of course not.

But it does mean you stop building your identity on what you don't have and start building it on what you do have, Christ.

Breaking the "incomplete" narrative isn't about convincing yourself you don't want a relationship. It's about refusing to let your worth be determined by whether you have one.

It's about saying, "I am whole today. And if someone joins my life tomorrow, they won't complete me, they'll walk beside someone who's already complete."

That shift changes everything.

Because when you know you're already full, you stop settling for crumbs.

MONDAY PRAYER

God, I've been living from the "incomplete" narrative.

I've told myself that my life will really begin when I meet someone. That I'll finally be whole when I'm in a relationship. That everything I'm waiting for is on the other side of being chosen.

But that's not true. And believing it has kept me stuck, chasing worth in people, waiting for circumstances to change before I'll let myself feel complete.

Forgive me for building my identity on what I don't have instead of on who I am in You. Forgive me for letting the world's definitions shape how I see myself. Forgive me for believing I'm incomplete when You've already made me full.

Break this narrative in me. Replace the lie with truth. Remind me that I am complete in Christ, not when someone shows up, but right now.

In Jesus' name, Amen.

TUESDAY PRAYER

Father, I don't know how to see myself as complete.

I've believed the "incomplete" story for so long that it feels true. When I look at my life, I see what's missing, not what's here. When I think about my future, I can only imagine it with someone else in it.

But that's not the life You've called me to. You've called me to fullness in You, regardless of my relationship status.

Teach me to see myself the way You see me. Not as lacking. Not as waiting. But as whole, complete, and fully loved right now.

Help me rewrite the narrative. Not with my circumstances, but with Your truth.

In Jesus' name, Amen.

WEDNESDAY PRAYER

Lord, I've been making decisions from a place of lack.

I've stayed in relationships longer than I should have because I was afraid of being alone. I've overlooked red flags because I didn't want to go back to feeling incomplete. I've compromised boundaries because I believed something was better than nothing.

But that's not how You want me to live. You want me to make decisions from a place of wholeness, not desperation. From security in You, not fear of being single.

Heal the broken foundation I've been building on. Teach me to stop settling for less because I believe I'm less. Teach me that I am complete in You, and that changes everything.

In Jesus' name, Amen.

THURSDAY PRAYER

God, help me stop waiting for someone to validate my worth.

I've been handing my identity over to people who were never meant to carry it. Every time someone didn't choose me, I took it as proof that I'm not enough. Every time a relationship ended, I felt like I lost a piece of myself.

But my worth isn't up for debate. It's not determined by who picks me or who walks away. It's determined by You, and You've already declared me complete.

Help me stop looking for validation in all the wrong places. Help me anchor my identity in You, not in whether someone sees my value. Help me believe that I am whole, whether anyone else notices or not.

In Jesus' name, Amen.

FRIDAY PRAYER

Father, I'm choosing to believe I'm complete.

Not because it feels true yet. Not because my circumstances reflect it. But because You say it, and Your Word is more reliable than my feelings.

I am complete in Christ. I am full because You've filled me. I am whole because You've made me so.

Help me live from that truth. Help me make decisions from that foundation. Help me stop waiting for someone to complete me and start walking as someone who's already whole.

This is the new narrative. And I'm choosing to believe it.

In Jesus' name, Amen.

SATURDAY PRAYER

God, thank You for breaking the "incomplete" narrative.

Thank You for reminding me that I'm not lacking. That I'm not half-formed. That I'm not waiting for someone to finish what You've already completed.

This week, You've been rewriting the story I've believed about myself. You've been replacing "incomplete" with "whole." You've been anchoring me in truth instead of lies.

Help me hold onto this. When the old narrative tries to come back, remind me of this week. Remind me that I am complete in Christ, and that's the only foundation I need.

In Jesus' name, Amen.

SUNDAY REFLECTION

Reflect:

- What decisions have you made from a place of feeling incomplete?

- What would change if you made decisions from a foundation of wholeness instead?

Declare:

- I am not incomplete.

- I am full in Christ.

- My worth is not determined by my relationship status.

> **Carry This: "For in Christ all the fullness of the Deity lives in bodily form, and in Christ you have been brought to fullness. He is the head over every power and authority.", Colossians 2:9-10 (NIV)**

SUNDAY PRAYER

God, I've been living from a broken foundation.

Building my identity on what I lack instead of on who I am in You. This week, You started rebuilding that foundation.

Help me keep building on truth. Help me make decisions from wholeness, not desperation. Help me believe that I'm complete in Christ.

In Jesus' name, Amen.

WEEK 11: HIS LOVE DOESN'T DEPEND ON YOUR RELATIONSHIP STATUS

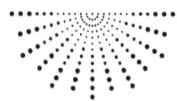

MONDAY DEVOTIONAL

You need to hear this, so I'm going to say it plainly:

God's love for you is not conditional on whether you're in a relationship.

He doesn't love you more when you're coupled. He doesn't love you less when you're single. His affection for you doesn't rise and fall based on your relationship status, your dating life, or whether someone has finally chosen you.

He loves you. Period.

Not because of what you have. Not because of who's beside you. Not because you've earned it or achieved it or proven yourself worthy of it.

He loves you because you're His.

And yet, you've been living like His love is tied to your circumstances. Like maybe, just maybe, if you were in a relationship, you'd feel more loved by God. More seen. More blessed. More favored.

But that's not how His love works.

Romans 8:38-39 says:

> "For I am convinced that neither death nor life, neither angels nor demons, neither the present nor the future, nor any powers, neither height nor depth, nor anything else in all creation, will be able to separate us from the love of God that is in Christ Jesus our Lord" (NIV).

Nothing can separate you from His love.

Not your singleness. Not your past relationships. Not your failed attempts at dating. Not the fact that you're still alone when you thought you'd be married by now.

Nothing.

God's love is not a reward for good behavior. It's not something you earn by being "ready enough" or "healed enough" or "spiritual enough." It's not something He grants when you finally meet someone.

It's already yours. Fully. Completely. Unconditionally.

The problem is, you've been measuring His love by your circumstances instead of by His character. You've been looking at your life and thinking, "If God really loved me, He would have brought someone by now."

But that logic doesn't work. Because if His love depended on your circumstances, it wouldn't be love, it would be a transaction.

God doesn't love you because your life is going well. He loves you because He's God. And His love doesn't change when your circumstances do.

You are not more loved when you're in a relationship.

You are not less loved when you're single.

You are loved. Fully. Completely. Unconditionally.

And that truth stands no matter what your life looks like.

MONDAY PRAYER

God, I've been measuring Your love by my circumstances.

When my life doesn't look the way I want it to, I assume You don't love me as much. When I'm still single and everyone else is moving forward, I question whether You really care about me.

But that's not who You are. Your love isn't conditional. It doesn't depend on whether I'm in a relationship or how "blessed" my life looks. It depends on who You are, and You are unchanging, faithful, and good.

Forgive me for doubting Your love. Forgive me for treating it like something I have to earn or something You withhold based on my circumstances. Forgive me for questioning Your heart toward me just because my life doesn't match my expectations.

Teach me to anchor my identity in Your love, not in my relationship status. Teach me that I am fully loved, whether I'm single or not.

In Jesus' name, Amen.

TUESDAY PRAYER

Father, I've felt unloved because I'm alone.

I know, logically, that You love me. But it's hard to feel it when I'm watching everyone else experience the kind of love I long for. It's hard to believe You care when You haven't answered this one prayer that feels so important to me.

But my feelings aren't the full picture. The truth is, You've never stopped loving me, not for a single moment. Not when I was at my worst. Not when I doubted You. Not when I was angry or distant or convinced You'd forgotten me.

Help me trust Your love even when I can't feel it. Help me believe that You're with me, You see me, and You care deeply about my life, whether or not my circumstances reflect that yet.

Your love for me is not in question. It never has been.

In Jesus' name, Amen.

WEDNESDAY PRAYER

Lord, I don't want to confuse Your love with my circumstances anymore.

I've been doing that for too long, assuming that if You loved me, my life would look different. That if You truly cared, You would have brought someone by now.

But that's not how love works. Your love isn't measured by whether You give me what I ask for. It's measured by the cross, where You gave everything for me before I ever asked.

You loved me when I was at my worst. You love me now, exactly as I am. And You'll love me tomorrow, no matter what changes or doesn't change.

Help me stop demanding proof of Your love through my circumstances. Help me rest in the proof You've already given, Jesus.

In Jesus' name, Amen.

THURSDAY PRAYER

God, I've been waiting to feel "blessed" before I believe You love me.

I've been looking at other people's lives, their relationships, their families, their seemingly perfect circumstances, and thinking, "That's what it looks like when God loves someone."

But that's not true. Your love isn't measured by blessings. It's measured by sacrifice. And You've already proven Your love for me in the most costly way possible.

Help me stop comparing my life to others' and assuming You love them more. Help me stop measuring Your affection by what I have or don't have. Help me believe that I am deeply, fully, completely loved, whether my life looks "blessed" or not.

In Jesus' name, Amen.

FRIDAY PRAYER

Father, anchor me in the truth of Your unchanging love.

Your love doesn't depend on my relationship status. It doesn't rise and fall with my circumstances. It doesn't change when my life does.

You loved me before I was born. You loved me at my worst. You love me today, exactly as I am. And You'll love me tomorrow, no matter what happens.

That's the foundation I need to stand on. Not my circumstances. Not my achievements. Not whether someone has chosen me.

Your love. Unchanging. Unshakable. Unconditional.

Help me live from that truth.

In Jesus' name, Amen.

SATURDAY PRAYER

God, thank You for loving me unconditionally.

Thank You for not tying Your love to my relationship status. Thank You for not requiring me to earn it or prove myself worthy of it. Thank You for loving me fully, completely, exactly as I am.

This week, You've reminded me that Your love doesn't depend on my circumstances. That I am not more loved when things are going well or less loved when things are hard. That Your love is constant, faithful, and unchanging.

Help me carry that truth forward. When I'm tempted to doubt Your love again, remind me of this week. Remind me that I am fully loved, always.

In Jesus' name, Amen.

SUNDAY REFLECTION

Reflect:

- Have you been measuring God's love by your circumstances? What would change if you stopped?

- What proof of God's love already exists in your life that you've been overlooking?

Declare:

- God's love for me is not conditional.

- I am fully loved, whether I'm in a relationship or not.

- Nothing can separate me from His love.

> **Carry This:** "Who shall separate us from the love of Christ? Shall trouble or hardship or persecution or famine or nakedness or danger or sword? ...No, in all these things we are more than conquerors through him who loved us.", Romans 8:35, 37 (NIV)

SUNDAY PRAYER

God, I've been measuring Your love by my circumstances.

Thinking that if You really loved me, my life would look different. But this week, You reminded me that Your love isn't conditional.

You loved me at the cross. That love doesn't change based on whether I'm single or married. Help me anchor my identity in that unchanging love.

In Jesus' name, Amen.

WEEK 12: THE GIFT OF UNDIVIDED DEVOTION

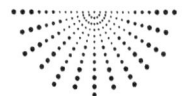

MONDAY DEVOTIONAL

This might be the hardest truth you'll read in this entire book:

Your singleness gives you something married people don't have, undivided devotion to God.

I know that sounds like a platitude. I know it sounds like something people say to make you feel better about being single. But hear me out, because this is real.

In 1 Corinthians 7:32-35, Paul writes something most Christians ignore because it's uncomfortable:

> "I would like you to be free from concern. An unmarried man is concerned about the Lord's affairs, how he can please the Lord. But a married man is concerned about the affairs of this world, how he can please his wife, and his interests are divided...I am saying this for your own good, not to restrict you, but that you may live in a right way in undivided devotion to the Lord" (NIV).

Undivided devotion.

That's what you have right now that you won't have in the same way if you get married.

Marriage is good. It's a gift. It's a beautiful reflection of Christ and the church. But it's also a responsibility that divides your attention. You can't pour yourself fully into God's work when you're also responsible for a spouse, a home, maybe kids.

That's not a bad thing, it's just a different thing.

Right now, you have time, energy, and attention that you can give fully to God. You can say yes to opportunities married people can't. You can go where they can't go. You can serve in ways they can't serve.

You have freedom.

And here's the hard truth: you might be spending that freedom wishing it away instead of using it.

You've been so focused on what you don't have that you've missed what you do have, a season where your heart, your time, and your devotion aren't divided.

That doesn't mean you're not allowed to desire marriage. It doesn't mean you have to love singleness. It doesn't mean you can't still pray for a partner.

But it does mean this: while you're here, steward the gift.

Don't waste this season wishing you were in the next one. Don't spend all your time resenting what you don't have. Don't let the longing for a relationship rob you of the opportunities this season provides.

Because one day, whether you get married or not, you'll look back on this time and either see wasted years or a season where you gave God your undivided attention.

The choice is yours.

MONDAY PRAYER

God, I've been resenting what You've been calling a gift.

I've looked at singleness as something to endure, not something to steward. I've focused so much on what I don't have that I've missed what I do have, undivided devotion to You.

Forgive me for wasting this season. Forgive me for treating it like a holding pattern instead of an opportunity. Forgive me for being so focused on the next chapter that I've missed what You're offering me in this one.

Teach me to steward this season well. Show me how to use the time, energy, and attention I have right now in ways that honor You. Help me see singleness not as a problem, but as a gift I can give back to You.

I don't want to waste this. Help me invest it wisely.

In Jesus' name, Amen.

TUESDAY PRAYER

Father, I've been too distracted to notice what You're offering.

I've spent so much time looking ahead, wondering when things will change, when someone will show up, when my life will look different, that I haven't been present in the season I'm actually in.

But You've given me something valuable right now: the ability to give You my full attention. No divided loyalties. No competing priorities. Just You and me.

Help me stop taking that for granted. Help me recognize the gift of undivided devotion and actually use it. Show me what You're calling me to do in this season that I wouldn't be able to do if my life looked different.

I don't want to look back and realize I missed it.

In Jesus' name, Amen.

WEDNESDAY PRAYER

Lord, show me what undivided devotion looks like for me.

I know You're calling me to something in this season, but I don't know what it is. I don't know where to pour my time, my energy, my heart. I don't know what You're asking me to do that only I can do right now.

So I'm asking You to show me. Reveal the opportunities I've been missing. Open doors I haven't seen. Give me clarity about how to steward this season in a way that honors You.

I have freedom right now. I have attention I can give fully to You. I don't want to waste it. Show me how to use it well.

In Jesus' name, Amen.

THURSDAY PRAYER

God, help me stop resenting the gift You've given me.

I've been treating undivided devotion like a consolation prize instead of a privilege. I've been so focused on what I'm missing that I haven't seen what I have.

But the truth is, this season is temporary. Whether I get married or stay single, I won't have this exact opportunity again. And I don't want to waste it wishing I was somewhere else.

Help me embrace this gift. Help me pour myself into what You're calling me to do right now, without holding back because I'm waiting for something better.

This season is a gift. And I'm choosing to treat it like one.

In Jesus' name, Amen.

FRIDAY PRAYER

Father, I'm releasing my timeline and embracing this season.

I don't know how long it will last. I don't know if I'll be single for another year, five years, or forever. But I do know this: while I'm here, I want to steward it well.

I want to give You my undivided attention. I want to say yes to the things You're calling me to that I won't be able to do if my circumstances change. I want to invest this season wisely instead of wishing it away.

Teach me what that looks like. Show me how to live fully in this season, even while I hope for something different.

In Jesus' name, Amen.

SATURDAY PRAYER

God, thank You for the gift of undivided devotion.

Thank You for this season, even when it's hard. Thank You for the freedom I have right now to pour myself fully into Your work. Thank You for the opportunities that come with singleness that I wouldn't have any other way.

This week, You've challenged me to stop resenting this season and start stewarding it. You've reminded me that undivided devotion is a gift, not a burden.

Help me live that out. Help me invest this season wisely. Help me look back one day and see that I used the time You gave me well.

In Jesus' name, Amen.

SUNDAY REFLECTION

Reflect:

- How have you been spending the freedom and undivided attention your singleness provides?

- What opportunities might God be offering you in this season that you've been missing?

Declare:

- My singleness is not a burden, it's a gift.

- I have undivided devotion to give to God right now.

- I will steward this season well.

> **Carry This:** "An unmarried woman or virgin is concerned about the Lord's affairs: Her aim is to be devoted to the Lord in both body and spirit.", 1 Corinthians 7:34b (NIV)

SUNDAY PRAYER

God, I've been resenting what You called a gift.

This week, You showed me that undivided devotion is an opportunity, not a burden. That this season offers something I won't have in the same way later.

Help me steward it well. Help me use this time, this freedom, this attention for Your purposes. I don't want to waste what You've given me.

In Jesus' name, Amen.

WEEK 13: ANCHORED IN CHRIST, NOT CIRCUMSTANCE

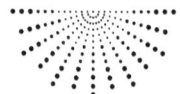

MONDAY DEVOTIONAL

Your circumstances will always change.

Relationships will begin and end. Jobs will come and go. Health will fluctuate. Plans will shift. Life will throw curveballs you didn't see coming.

And if your identity, your peace, and your worth are tied to any of that, you'll spend your entire life feeling unstable.

That's why this matters:

You cannot anchor your life in circumstances. You have to anchor it in Christ.

Hebrews 6:19 says:

> "We have this hope as an anchor for the soul, firm and secure" (NIV).

An anchor.

Not a suggestion. Not a nice idea. An anchor, the thing that keeps you steady when the storm hits. The thing that keeps you from drifting when the current pulls. The thing that holds you in place when everything around you is chaos.

And that anchor isn't a relationship. It's not a job. It's not success, approval, or having your life figured out.

It's Christ.

Here's the reality: if you're anchored in your circumstances, you'll panic every time they shift. If being single is the worst thing that can happen to you, you'll live in constant fear of staying that way. If your peace depends on meeting someone, you'll never actually have peace, because even if you meet someone, you'll just transfer the anxiety to keeping them.

But if you're anchored in Christ, your circumstances can change without shattering you.

You can be single and steady.

You can be disappointed and not destroyed.

You can hope for something different while still finding peace in what is.

Because your stability doesn't come from what's happening around you. It comes from who's holding you.

Look, this isn't easy. It's not a one-time decision. It's a daily, sometimes hourly, choice to say, "My worth, my peace, and my identity are not determined by whether I have what I want. They're determined by whose I am."

And on your worst days, when singleness feels unbearable, when you're watching another friend get engaged, when you're wondering if God has forgotten you, that anchor is what keeps you from drifting into bitterness, despair, or compromise.

You are held. Not by circumstances. Not by relationships. Not by how well your life is going.

You are held by Christ.

And that's the only anchor that will never fail.

MONDAY PRAYER

God, I've been anchored in the wrong things.

I've tied my peace to my circumstances. I've tied my worth to my relationship status. I've tied my stability to whether my life looks the way I thought it would.

And every time something shifts, I fall apart.

Forgive me for building my life on unstable ground. Forgive me for looking to circumstances to give me what only You can give. Forgive me for treating my relationship status like the anchor when it was never meant to hold that weight.

Teach me to anchor myself in You. Not in what I have. Not in what I hope for. But in who You are, unchanging, faithful, steady.

I want to be anchored in Christ, not circumstance. Help me make that shift.

In Jesus' name, Amen.

TUESDAY PRAYER

Father, I'm tired of being tossed around by my circumstances.

One day I'm okay. The next day I'm falling apart. One moment I feel hopeful. The next I'm drowning in despair. And it all depends on what's happening around me, who's getting engaged, who's moving forward, whether I'm closer to what I want or further away.

But I wasn't meant to live like this. I wasn't meant to be at the mercy of circumstances.

Anchor me in You. Anchor me in truth that doesn't change when my life does. Anchor me in a foundation that holds, no matter what storm I'm facing.

I don't want my peace to depend on my circumstances. I want it to depend on You.

In Jesus' name, Amen.

WEDNESDAY PRAYER

Lord, teach me what it means to be anchored in Christ.

I know the words. I know the theology. But I don't always know how to live it.

Show me what it looks like to find stability in You when everything around me feels unstable. Show me how to trust You when my circumstances don't reflect Your promises. Show me how to rest in who You are when I can't see what You're doing.

I want to be rooted, grounded, anchored, not in what I have, but in who You are.

Teach me what that looks like in real life, on the hard days, when I can't feel You.

In Jesus' name, Amen.

THURSDAY PRAYER

God, help me stop panicking every time my circumstances shift.

I've been living in constant fear, fear that things won't change, fear that they will change and I won't be ready, fear that I'm missing something, fear that I'm falling behind.

But fear is not the life You've called me to. You've called me to peace that surpasses understanding. Peace that holds even when nothing makes sense.

Anchor me in that peace. Remind me that my circumstances don't determine my worth. That disappointment doesn't disqualify me. That setbacks don't mean You've abandoned me.

I am held. And that's enough.

In Jesus' name, Amen.

FRIDAY PRAYER

Father, I'm choosing to anchor myself in You.

Not in my timeline. Not in my plans. Not in whether my life looks the way I hoped.

In You.

Your love. Your promises. Your faithfulness. Your character.

Those things don't change when my circumstances do. Those things don't shift when life gets hard. Those things are steady, reliable, unshakable.

Help me build my life on that foundation. Help me stop looking to circumstances for stability and start looking to You.

I am anchored in Christ. And that's the only foundation I need.

In Jesus' name, Amen.

SATURDAY PRAYER

God, thank You for being my anchor.

Thank You for holding me steady when everything around me feels chaotic. Thank You for being the foundation that doesn't shift, the truth that doesn't change, the love that doesn't fail.

This week, You've reminded me that I can't anchor my life in circumstances, I have to anchor it in You. You've challenged me to stop tying my peace to what's happening around me and start tying it to who's holding me.

Help me live from that truth. When I'm tempted to panic, remind me that I'm anchored in Christ. When circumstances shift, remind me that You don't.

I am held. And that changes everything.

In Jesus' name, Amen.

SUNDAY REFLECTION

Reflect:

- What circumstances have you been using as anchors that were never meant to hold that weight?

- What would change if you anchored your identity, peace, and worth in Christ instead?

Declare:

- I am anchored in Christ, not circumstance.

- My peace does not depend on my relationship status.

- I am held by God, and that is enough.

> **Carry This:** "We have this hope as an anchor for the soul, firm and secure. It enters the inner sanctuary behind the curtain, where our forerunner, Jesus, has entered on our behalf.", Hebrews 6:19-20a (NIV)

SUNDAY PRAYER

God, I've been anchored in the wrong things.

Tying my peace to my circumstances, my worth to my relationship status. This week, You reminded me that the only anchor that holds is You.

Help me stay anchored in Christ. When circumstances shift, when storms come, when everything around me changes, help me remember that You don't.

In Jesus' name, Amen.

WEEK 14: THE WOUNDS THAT STILL ACHE

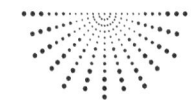

MONDAY DEVOTIONAL

You can't heal what you won't acknowledge.

That's the hard truth about wounds, especially the ones from past relationships. You can bury them. You can ignore them. You can pretend they don't affect you anymore. But until you actually face them, name them, and bring them to God, they'll keep shaping your life in ways you don't even realize.

Maybe it was the person who led you on for months and then chose someone else. Maybe it was the relationship that ended suddenly with no real explanation. Maybe it was the one who made you feel like you were never quite enough. Maybe it was the pattern of being the "backup plan" instead of the first choice.

Whatever it was, it left a mark.

And you've been carrying it longer than you should.

Psalm 147:3 says:

> "He heals the brokenhearted and binds up their wounds" (NIV).

Notice it doesn't say He heals the people who pretend they're fine. It says He heals the brokenhearted, the ones who admit they're hurt. The ones who bring their wounds to Him instead of hiding them.

God can't heal what you won't give Him.

Here's what happens when you leave wounds unhealed: they become patterns. You start protecting yourself in ways that keep you from ever being truly vulnerable again. You build walls. You sabotage good things before they can hurt you. You assume the worst about people before they have a chance to prove otherwise.

And you tell yourself it's wisdom. You tell yourself it's being smart, being careful, not getting hurt again.

But it's not wisdom. It's fear. And fear dressed up as caution will keep you from ever experiencing the kind of love you actually want.

Healing doesn't mean the hurt never happened. It doesn't mean you forget what was done to you. It doesn't mean you excuse bad behavior or pretend it didn't matter.

Healing means you stop letting the past control your future.

It means you acknowledge the wound, bring it to God, and let Him do what only He can do, bind it up, restore what was broken, and make you whole again.

Not so you can jump into another relationship. Not so you can prove you're "over it." But so you can move forward without dragging the weight of unhealed pain behind you.

The wounds are there. You know they are.

It's time to stop ignoring them and start healing them.

MONDAY PRAYER

God, I've been pretending I'm fine when I'm not.

I've buried wounds I should have brought to You. I've acted like the past doesn't affect me anymore, but it does. I can feel it in the way I protect myself, the way I assume the worst, the way I keep people at arm's length.

I'm tired of carrying this pain. I'm tired of pretending it doesn't exist. I'm tired of letting old wounds dictate how I show up in new situations.

So I'm bringing them to You. All of them. The rejections. The betrayals. The times I was led on, used, discarded. The relationships that left me feeling like I was never enough.

Heal me, Lord. Not just surface-level, but deep. Bind up the wounds I've been hiding. Restore what was broken. Help me stop protecting myself in ways that keep me from truly living.

I can't heal myself. But You can.

In Jesus' name, Amen.

TUESDAY PRAYER

Father, some wounds still ache.

I thought I was over them. I thought time had healed them. But then something triggers the memory, and I realize I've just been ignoring the pain instead of dealing with it.

I don't want to live like this anymore. I don't want old wounds controlling my present. I don't want past hurts determining my future.

Show me what still needs healing. Bring to the surface the wounds I've been avoiding. Help me face them honestly, without shame, without pretending they're smaller than they are.

You are the healer. And I'm trusting You to do what I can't, make me whole again.

In Jesus' name, Amen.

WEDNESDAY PRAYER

Lord, I don't want to bring these wounds into my next relationship.

I know what happens when people enter relationships before they've healed. I've seen it. I've maybe even done it. And I don't want to repeat that pattern.

I don't want to punish someone new for what someone old did to me. I don't want to build walls that keep out good people because bad people hurt me. I don't want to sabotage something healthy because I'm still carrying pain from something toxic.

Heal me first. Make me whole before I invite someone into my life. Help me deal with the wounds now so I don't drag them into my future.

I want to be ready, not perfect, but healed.

In Jesus' name, Amen.

THURSDAY PRAYER

God, help me stop protecting wounds instead of healing them.

I've built my entire life around not getting hurt again. I've created rules, walls, and defenses all designed to keep pain out. And in the process, I've kept love out too.

But protecting wounds doesn't heal them. It just keeps them fresh.

Teach me the difference between wisdom and fear. Teach me how to be vulnerable again without being reckless. Teach me how to guard my heart without hardening it.

I don't want to live in fear of being hurt. I want to live in freedom, knowing that even if pain comes again, You'll heal me then too.

In Jesus' name, Amen.

FRIDAY PRAYER

Father, I'm ready to let go.

I've been holding onto wounds longer than I needed to. I've replayed conversations, relived moments, rehearsed what I should have said or done differently. I've kept the pain alive by refusing to release it.

But I'm done. I'm ready to let go.

Not because I'm excusing what happened. Not because it didn't matter. But because holding onto it is hurting me more than it's hurting anyone else.

I release the pain. I release the bitterness. I release the people who hurt me. And I'm asking You to heal what they broke.

I'm ready to move forward, whole.

In Jesus' name, Amen.

SATURDAY PRAYER

God, I brought You wounds I've been hiding for years.

Some of them I didn't even realize were still there. Some of them I thought had healed but were just buried.

You've started something this week, binding up what's been broken, bringing light to what I kept in darkness.

Don't let me bury them again. Don't let me go back to pretending I'm fine when I'm not.

Finish what You started. I'm trusting You to complete the healing.

In Jesus' name, Amen.

SUNDAY REFLECTION

Reflect:

- What wounds from past relationships are you still carrying?

- What would it look like to bring those wounds to God instead of protecting them?

Declare:

- I will not carry wounds God wants to heal.

- I am bringing my pain to the Healer.

- I am being made whole.

> **Carry This:** "He heals the brokenhearted and binds up their wounds.", Psalm 147:3 (NIV)

SUNDAY PRAYER

God, I brought You wounds this week that I've been hiding for too long.

Wounds I thought had healed but were just buried. And You started binding them up, bringing light to what I kept in darkness.

Don't let me bury them again. Finish what You started. I'm trusting You to complete the healing.

In Jesus' name, Amen.

WEEK 15: FORGIVING THE ONE WHO HURT YOU

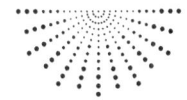

MONDAY DEVOTIONAL

Forgiveness is not optional.

I know that's hard to hear, especially when you're still processing the hurt. Especially when the wound is fresh. Especially when the person who hurt you hasn't apologized, hasn't changed, hasn't even acknowledged what they did.

But here's the truth:

Unforgiveness will destroy you faster than the person who hurt you ever could.

It's poison. And the longer you hold onto it, the more damage it does, not to them, but to you.

Jesus didn't make forgiveness a suggestion. He made it a command. In Matthew 6:14-15, He says:

> "For if you forgive other people when they sin against you, your heavenly Father will also forgive you. But if you do not forgive others their sins, your Father will not forgive your sins" (NIV).

That's not gentle. That's not a nice idea. That's a direct statement: forgive, or you're blocking your own relationship with God.

Now, let's be clear about what forgiveness is and what it's not.

Forgiveness is not saying what they did was okay. It's not excusing their behavior. It's not pretending it didn't hurt. It's not letting them back into your life like nothing happened.

Forgiveness is releasing your right to revenge. It's choosing to let go of the bitterness. It's refusing to let what they did to you define the rest of your life.

You forgive for you, not for them.

Because as long as you're holding onto unforgiveness, you're still tied to them. You're still giving them power over your emotions, your peace, your future. Every time you replay what they did, every time you imagine what you should have said, every time you fantasize about them getting what they deserve, you're letting them control you.

Forgiveness cuts that cord.

It doesn't mean the hurt disappears overnight. It doesn't mean you won't feel angry sometimes. It doesn't mean you have to trust them again.

It just means you're choosing freedom over bitterness. Healing over hatred. Your future over their past.

And here's the hardest part: you might have to forgive them over and over again.

Because forgiveness isn't always a one-time event. Sometimes it's a daily choice. Sometimes you wake up and the anger is back, and you have to choose forgiveness again.

But every time you choose it, you take back a piece of your life that they stole.

Forgiveness doesn't make them right. It makes you free.

MONDAY PRAYER

God, I don't want to forgive them.

I want them to hurt the way they hurt me. I want them to feel the pain they caused. I want justice, consequences, acknowledgment, something that proves what they did mattered.

But holding onto that is destroying me. I can feel it. The bitterness. The anger. The constant replaying of what happened. It's poisoning my peace, my relationships, my ability to move forward.

So I'm choosing to forgive. Not because they deserve it. Not because what they did was okay. But because I deserve freedom more than I deserve revenge.

I release them. I release the debt they owe me. I release my right to make them pay for what they did.

I'm choosing forgiveness. Not for them. For me.

Help me mean it. Help me walk in it. Help me keep choosing it, even when the anger comes back.

In Jesus' name, Amen.

TUESDAY PRAYER

Father, forgiveness feels impossible.

How do I forgive someone who hasn't even apologized? How do I let go when they've never acknowledged the damage they caused? How do I release someone who's moved on like nothing happened while I'm still picking up the pieces?

It feels unfair. It feels like I'm letting them off the hook.

But I know unforgiveness is a heavier burden than they'll ever carry. And I'm tired of carrying it.

So I'm asking You to do what I can't. Give me the strength to forgive when I don't feel like it. Give me the grace to release them when everything in me wants to hold on. Give me the freedom that comes from letting go.

I can't do this on my own. But with You, I can.

In Jesus' name, Amen.

WEDNESDAY PRAYER

Lord, help me separate forgiveness from trust.

I'm afraid that if I forgive them, I have to let them back in. That forgiveness means pretending it never happened. That releasing the offense means opening the door to more pain.

But that's not what You're asking.

You're asking me to forgive, to release the bitterness, to stop letting the past control me. But You're not asking me to be foolish. Forgiveness doesn't require reconciliation. It doesn't demand I trust someone who's proven untrustworthy.

I can forgive and still have boundaries. I can release them and still protect myself. I can choose freedom without choosing foolishness.

Teach me that balance. Teach me how to forgive fully while still guarding wisely.

In Jesus' name, Amen.

THURSDAY PRAYER

God, I keep replaying what happened.

Over and over. I imagine what I should have said. I rehearse the confrontation I'll never have. I fantasize about them realizing what they lost, what they did, how badly they messed up.

But none of that is helping me. It's just keeping the wound open.

Help me stop. Help me stop giving them space in my head. Help me stop letting them control my thoughts, my emotions, my peace.

I'm choosing to release them, not just in words, but in my mind. Every time the replay starts, I'm going to choose forgiveness again. Every time the bitterness rises, I'm going to choose freedom.

They don't get to live rent-free in my head anymore.

In Jesus' name, Amen.

FRIDAY PRAYER

Father, I'm forgiving them today.

Not because they've earned it. Not because they've apologized. Not because I feel like it.

But because You forgave me when I didn't deserve it. Because You released my debt when I couldn't pay it. Because You chose mercy over justice, and You're asking me to do the same.

So I'm letting go. I'm releasing the anger. I'm choosing freedom over bitterness.

I forgive them. Fully. Completely. Not because of who they are, but because of who You are.

Help me keep walking in this. When the anger resurfaces, remind me of this moment. Remind me that I already chose freedom.

In Jesus' name, Amen.

SATURDAY PRAYER

God, I chose freedom this week.

Freedom over bitterness. Freedom over revenge. Freedom over the prison I built trying to punish someone who probably never even noticed.

And even though it's hard, even though the anger will probably try to come back, I already feel the weight lifting.

Keep me free. When I'm tempted to pick up what I put down, stop me. Remind me how heavy it was.

In Jesus' name, Amen.

SUNDAY REFLECTION

Reflect:

- Who do you need to forgive that you've been holding onto?

- What would freedom look like if you released the unforgiveness today?

Declare:

- I am choosing forgiveness over bitterness.

- I am releasing those who hurt me.

- I am free.

> **Carry This:** "Bear with each other and forgive one another if any of you has a grievance against someone. Forgive as the Lord forgave you.", Colossians 3:13 (NIV)

SUNDAY PRAYER

God, I chose freedom this week.

Freedom over bitterness, over revenge, over the prison I built trying to punish someone who probably never even noticed. And even though it's hard, I already feel the weight lifting.

Help me stay free. When the anger tries to come back, remind me how heavy it was. I'm done carrying it.

In Jesus' name, Amen.

WEEK 16: FORGIVING YOURSELF

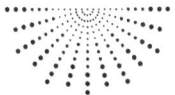

MONDAY DEVOTIONAL

You've forgiven them. But you haven't forgiven yourself.

That's the one people forget. You release the person who hurt you, you let go of the bitterness, you choose freedom, and then you turn all that anger inward.

You replay your mistakes. You beat yourself up for not seeing the red flags sooner. You condemn yourself for the choices you made, the boundaries you didn't set, the times you stayed when you should have left.

And you tell yourself you deserved it. That it was your fault. That if you had just been smarter, stronger, better, it wouldn't have happened.

But here's the truth:

You didn't deserve to be hurt. And punishing yourself won't change what happened.

Romans 8:1 says:

"Therefore, there is now no condemnation for those who are in Christ Jesus" (NIV).

No condemnation.

Not "a little bit of condemnation." Not "condemnation when you really mess up." No condemnation.

If God doesn't condemn you, why are you condemning yourself?

You made mistakes. You trusted the wrong person. You ignored red flags. You stayed too long. You gave too much. You believed lies. You compromised boundaries you shouldn't have.

You're human.

And being human means you're going to make mistakes. It means you're going to trust people who don't deserve it. It means you're going to misread situations, overlook warnings, and give your heart to people who break it.

That doesn't make you stupid. It doesn't make you weak. It doesn't make you unworthy of love.

It makes you someone who took a risk. Someone who was brave enough to be vulnerable. Someone who loved, even when it cost you.

And yes, you learned hard lessons. Yes, there are things you'll do differently next time. Yes, you wish you could go back and make better choices.

But you can't. And torturing yourself over what you can't change is just another form of bondage.

God has already forgiven you. He's already washed you clean. He's already declared you righteous, holy, blameless in His sight.

The only person still holding your past against you is you.

And it's time to let that go.

Not because you're excusing your mistakes. Not because you're pretending they didn't matter. But because you're choosing to receive the grace God has already given you.

Forgive yourself. Not because you deserve it any more than the person who hurt you did. But because holding onto self-condemnation is just as poisonous as holding onto unforgiveness.

You've already been forgiven. Now it's time to believe it.

MONDAY PRAYER

God, I've been harder on myself than I've been on anyone else.

I've forgiven people who hurt me, but I haven't forgiven myself. I replay my mistakes on a loop. I punish myself for not knowing better, not doing better, not being better.

But You've already forgiven me. You've already washed me clean. You've already declared me righteous in Christ.

So why am I still condemning myself?

Forgive me for rejecting the grace You've already given me. Forgive me for holding onto guilt You've already removed. Forgive me for punishing myself for mistakes You've already covered.

Teach me to forgive myself the way You've forgiven me, fully, completely, without condition.

I am not condemned. And I'm choosing to believe that today.

In Jesus' name, Amen.

TUESDAY PRAYER

Father, I wish I had done things differently.

I wish I had seen the red flags sooner. I wish I had protected myself better. I wish I had walked away when I should have instead of staying and getting hurt.

But I can't change the past. And beating myself up over it isn't helping me move forward.

Help me let go of the "what ifs." Help me stop torturing myself over decisions I can't undo. Help me accept that I did the best I could with what I knew at the time.

I made mistakes. But I'm not defined by them. I'm defined by Your grace.

Help me walk in that truth.

In Jesus' name, Amen.

WEDNESDAY PRAYER

Lord, I don't know how to stop punishing myself.

Every time I think I've moved on, something triggers the memory and I'm right back there, replaying what I did wrong, how I could have prevented it, why I wasn't smarter.

But this isn't conviction. This is condemnation. And condemnation doesn't come from You.

Teach me the difference. Teach me to receive correction without drowning in shame. Teach me to learn from my mistakes without being defined by them.

I am not my worst moment. I am not my biggest failure. I am not the sum of my mistakes.

I am Yours. And that's the only identity that matters.

In Jesus' name, Amen.

THURSDAY PRAYER

God, help me extend to myself the grace I extend to others.

I would never talk to someone else the way I talk to myself. I would never condemn them the way I condemn myself. I would never hold their past against them the way I hold mine against me.

So why do I think it's okay to treat myself this way?

Teach me to be as kind to myself as I am to others. Teach me to offer myself the same grace, the same patience, the same forgiveness I freely give to everyone else.

I am not the exception to Your grace. I am covered by it, just like everyone else.

Help me believe that.

In Jesus' name, Amen.

FRIDAY PRAYER

Father, I'm choosing to forgive myself today.

Not because my mistakes didn't matter. Not because I'm excusing what I did. But because You've already forgiven me, and I'm choosing to receive that.

I forgive myself for the choices I wish I hadn't made. I forgive myself for staying too long, giving too much, ignoring the warnings. I forgive myself for being human.

I release the guilt. I release the shame. I release the self-condemnation.

I am forgiven. And I'm choosing to walk in that freedom.

In Jesus' name, Amen.

SATURDAY PRAYER

God, this was the hardest one.

Forgiving myself. Believing You've actually released what I keep holding against myself.

But I did it. I spoke it out loud. I let it go.

Now help me live like someone who's been forgiven. Not perfectly, I know I'll stumble. But like someone who actually believes Your grace is real.

In Jesus' name, Amen.

SUNDAY REFLECTION

Reflect:

- What are you still punishing yourself for that God has already forgiven?

- What would change if you extended to yourself the same grace you extend to others?

Declare:

- I am not condemned.

- I am forgiven.

- I am free.

> **Carry This:** "Therefore, there is now no condemnation for those who are in Christ Jesus.", Romans 8:1 (NIV)

SUNDAY PRAYER

God, forgiving myself was harder than forgiving them.

But I did it. I spoke it out loud. I let it go. And I'm choosing to believe that Your grace actually covers what I've been holding against myself.

Help me live like someone who's been forgiven. Not perfectly, but like someone who believes Your mercy is real.

In Jesus' name, Amen.

WEEK 17: BREAKING UNHEALTHY RELATIONSHIP PATTERNS

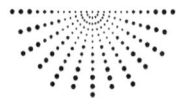

MONDAY DEVOTIONAL

You keep choosing the same type of person.

Different name. Different face. Different job. But the same patterns. The same red flags. The same ending.

And every time it happens, you tell yourself, "This time will be different."

But it's not. Because you're not.

Here's the hard truth: if you don't break the pattern, the pattern will keep breaking you.

You can't keep doing the same thing and expecting different results. You can't keep choosing emotionally unavailable people and hoping they'll suddenly become emotionally present. You can't keep ignoring red flags and expecting green lights.

Something has to change. And that something is you.

Not because you're broken. Not because you're the problem. But because you're the only variable you can control.

In Proverbs 26:11, it says:

> "As a dog returns to its vomit, so fools repeat their folly" (NIV).

That's harsh. But it's true.

Going back to the same patterns, the same types of people, the same toxic dynamics, that's folly. And God is asking you to be wise enough to stop.

So why do we do it? Why do we keep repeating the same mistakes?

Sometimes it's familiarity. We're drawn to what we know, even when what we know is unhealthy. We mistake intensity for intimacy, chaos for chemistry, and we convince ourselves that "fixing" someone will prove our worth.

Sometimes it's unhealed wounds. We're trying to rewrite the past by choosing people who remind us of the ones who hurt us, hoping that this time, we can get a different ending.

Sometimes it's low self-worth. We don't believe we deserve better, so we settle for what feels familiar, even when it's damaging.

But here's what you need to understand:

Healing the wound is more important than finding the relationship.

If you don't break the pattern now, you'll just drag it into the next relationship. And the one after that. And the one after that.

So how do you break it?

You start by identifying it. What type of person do you keep choosing? What red flags do you keep ignoring? What role do you keep playing?

Then you ask God to heal whatever wound is driving the pattern. Because patterns aren't random. They're protective mechanisms, coping strategies, trauma responses, something in you believes this is what love looks like, and that belief needs to be healed.

And then you make different choices. Even when it feels uncomfortable. Even when "different" doesn't feel as exciting as "familiar." Even when the healthier option doesn't give you the same adrenaline rush as the toxic one.

You choose different. Over and over. Until different becomes your new normal.

Breaking the pattern isn't easy. But staying in it is harder.

MONDAY PRAYER

God, I keep choosing the same type of person.

Different name, same pattern. Different relationship, same ending. And I'm tired of it.

I don't want to keep repeating the same mistakes. I don't want to drag the same toxic patterns into every relationship I enter. I don't want to look back in five years and realize nothing has changed because I haven't changed.

Show me the pattern. Help me see it clearly, the types of people I'm drawn to, the red flags I ignore, the role I keep playing. Bring it to the surface so I can finally deal with it.

And then heal whatever wound is driving it. Heal the part of me that thinks this is what love looks like. Heal the part of me that's drawn to chaos, intensity, or unavailability.

I want to break the pattern. Help me do what I can't do on my own.

In Jesus' name, Amen.

TUESDAY PRAYER

Father, I've been confusing intensity with intimacy.

I've mistaken chaos for chemistry. I've confused someone pursuing me aggressively with someone actually loving me well. I've believed that if it doesn't feel overwhelming, it's not real.

But that's not love. That's adrenaline. And I've been addicted to it.

Teach me what healthy love actually looks like. Teach me that steady doesn't mean boring. That peace doesn't mean passionless. That someone being consistent and reliable is actually more valuable than someone being intense and unpredictable.

Rewire my understanding of love. Help me stop chasing the high and start building something real.

In Jesus' name, Amen.

WEDNESDAY PRAYER

Lord, I keep ignoring red flags.

I see them. I know they're there. But I talk myself out of them. I make excuses. I convince myself it's not that bad, or that they'll change, or that I'm being too picky.

But red flags are warnings. And ignoring them doesn't make them go away, it just guarantees I'll regret it later.

Give me the courage to walk away when I see the signs. Give me the wisdom to trust my gut instead of overriding it. Give me the strength to choose what's healthy over what's familiar.

I don't want to ignore red flags anymore. I want to honor them.

In Jesus' name, Amen.

THURSDAY PRAYER

God, I've been trying to fix people.

I've believed that if I just love them enough, they'll change. That if I'm patient enough, supportive enough, understanding enough, they'll become the person I need them to be.

But that's not my job. And it's not working.

I can't fix anyone. I can't change anyone. I can't love someone into wholeness when they're not willing to do the work themselves.

Help me stop playing savior. Help me stop choosing broken people and trying to heal them. Help me recognize that someone else's potential is not the same as their reality.

I want to choose someone who's already doing the work, not someone I'm hoping will start.

In Jesus' name, Amen.

FRIDAY PRAYER

Father, help me make different choices.

I know what the pattern is. I know what I need to break. But knowing and doing are two different things.

When I'm tempted to go back to what's familiar, give me the strength to choose different. When I'm drawn to the same type of person, remind me why I can't go there again. When the old pattern tries to pull me back, anchor me in truth.

Breaking this pattern is going to feel uncomfortable. It's going to feel wrong, even when it's right. But I'm choosing it anyway.

Help me stay the course. Help me choose health over familiarity, even when it's hard.

In Jesus' name, Amen.

SATURDAY PRAYER

God, I see it now.

The pattern I couldn't see before. The wound that's been driving my choices. The reason I keep ending up in the same place with different people.

Seeing it doesn't fix it overnight. But it's the beginning.

Give me strength to do the work. To heal what needs healing. To choose differently even when different feels wrong.

In Jesus' name, Amen.

SUNDAY REFLECTION

Reflect:

- What unhealthy relationship pattern keeps showing up in your life?

- What wound might be driving that pattern, and how can you bring it to God for healing?

Declare:

- I am breaking unhealthy patterns.

- I am making different choices.

- I deserve healthy, whole love.

> Carry This: "As a dog returns to its vomit, so fools repeat their folly.", Proverbs 26:11 (NIV)

SUNDAY PRAYER

God, I see the pattern now.

The wound that's been driving my choices, the reason I keep ending up in the same place with different people. Seeing it doesn't fix it overnight, but it's the beginning.

Give me strength to do the work. To heal what needs healing. To choose differently even when different feels wrong.

In Jesus' name, Amen.

WEEK 18: WHEN PAST REJECTION STILL SPEAKS

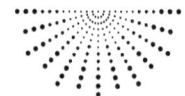

MONDAY DEVOTIONAL

Rejection has a voice.

And if you're not careful, you'll let it narrate your entire life.

It whispers when you're getting close to someone new: "They'll leave too."

It shouts when you're thinking about being vulnerable: "Don't. You'll just get hurt again."

It drowns out hope with fear: "Why even try? You know how this ends."

Past rejection doesn't just hurt in the moment, it echoes. It shapes how you see yourself, how you approach relationships, and whether you believe you're actually worthy of being chosen.

And until you silence that voice, it will sabotage every good thing that comes your way.

Here's what rejection does: it takes a specific moment, one person, one situation, one painful experience, and turns it into a universal truth about who you are.

One person rejected you, and now you believe everyone will.

One relationship ended badly, and now you assume all relationships will.

One person didn't see your value, and now you question whether you have any.

But rejection is not truth. It's just an experience. A painful one, yes. But it's not a prophecy about your future or a verdict on your worth.

Isaiah 54:4 says:

> **"Do not be afraid; you will not be put to shame. Do not fear disgrace; you will not be humiliated. You will forget the shame of your youth and remember no more the reproach of your widowhood" (NIV).**

You will forget the shame.

Not because it didn't hurt. Not because it didn't matter. But because God is bigger than the voice of rejection, and His voice gets the final say.

The person who rejected you doesn't get to define you. The relationship that ended doesn't get to determine your worth. The people who walked away don't get to write the rest of your story.

They rejected you. They didn't disqualify you.

And there's a massive difference.

So how do you silence the voice of rejection?

You replace it with truth. Every time rejection whispers, "You're not enough," you counter it with, "God says I am." Every time it says, "No one will choose you," you respond with, "God already has."

You stop giving past rejection power over your present. You stop letting one person's decision dictate your entire identity. You stop replaying the rejection and start rewriting the narrative.

Rejection happened. But it's not who you are.

And it's time to stop letting it speak for you.

MONDAY PRAYER

God, past rejection still has a voice in my life.

It tells me I'm not enough. It tells me I'll never be chosen. It tells me that what happened before will happen again, so why even try?

And I've been listening to it. I've been letting it shape my decisions, my relationships, my belief about what I deserve.

But rejection is not truth. It's just an experience. A painful one, but not a prophecy.

Silence that voice. Replace it with Yours. Remind me that one person's rejection doesn't define my worth. That one failed relationship doesn't determine my future. That being overlooked doesn't mean I'm unworthy.

Help me stop replaying the rejection and start believing the truth, I am chosen, I am loved, I am enough.

In Jesus' name, Amen.

TUESDAY PRAYER

Father, I'm afraid of being rejected again.

So I protect myself. I keep people at a distance. I don't let anyone get too close because I can't handle the thought of going through that pain again.

But living in fear of rejection isn't living, it's surviving. And I don't want to spend the rest of my life afraid.

Help me separate past rejection from future possibility. Help me stop assuming that because one person walked away, everyone will. Help me be brave enough to be vulnerable again, even when it scares me.

Rejection happened. But it's not guaranteed to happen again. And even if it does, I'll survive it, because You'll be with me.

In Jesus' name, Amen.

WEDNESDAY PRAYER

Lord, I've internalized the rejection.

I've taken what one person said or did and made it my identity. I've believed their decision to walk away was proof that something is fundamentally wrong with me.

But that's not true. Their rejection says more about them than it does about me. Their inability to see my value doesn't mean I don't have any.

Help me stop carrying their rejection as my identity. Help me separate their decision from my worth. Help me believe that I am valuable, even when someone else couldn't see it.

I am not defined by who rejected me. I am defined by who chose me, You.

In Jesus' name, Amen.

THURSDAY PRAYER

God, help me stop punishing new people for what old people did.

I know I do it. I assume the worst. I expect them to leave. I build walls before they even have a chance to prove themselves.

But that's not fair to them. And it's not fair to me.

Teach me to give people a fair chance. Teach me that not everyone is like the ones who hurt me. Teach me that past rejection doesn't predict future outcomes.

I want to be open again. I want to trust again. I want to believe that good people exist and that I'm capable of experiencing healthy love.

Help me stop letting past rejection ruin present possibilities.

In Jesus' name, Amen.

FRIDAY PRAYER

Father, I'm releasing the voice of rejection.

I'm done letting it narrate my life. I'm done replaying what was said, what was done, how I was discarded. I'm done giving those moments more power than they deserve.

Rejection happened. But it's over. And I'm choosing to move forward without it.

I release the people who rejected me. I release the shame I've carried. I release the lies I've believed about my worth.

I am not rejected. I am chosen. And that's the voice I'm listening to from now on.

In Jesus' name, Amen.

SATURDAY PRAYER

God, You gave rejection a voice for too long.

This week, I started learning to silence it. Started replacing lies with truth. Started believing that one person's decision doesn't get to narrate my entire story.

The voice will try to come back. I know it will.

But now I have something stronger, Your voice. And when they speak at the same time, I'm choosing to listen to You.

In Jesus' name, Amen.

SUNDAY REFLECTION

Reflect:

- What voice of past rejection are you still listening to?

- How would your life change if you stopped letting past rejection predict your future?

Declare:

- Past rejection does not define me.

- I am chosen by God.

- I will not let fear of rejection keep me from living fully.

> **Carry This: "Do not be afraid; you will not be put to shame. Do not fear disgrace; you will not be humiliated.", Isaiah 54:4a (NIV)**

SUNDAY PRAYER

God, I gave rejection a voice for too long.

This week, I started learning to silence it. Started replacing lies with truth. Started believing that one person's decision doesn't get to narrate my entire story.

The voice will try to come back. But now I have something stronger. Your voice. And when they speak at the same time, I'm choosing to listen to You.

In Jesus' name, Amen.

WEEK 19: GUARDING YOUR HEART WITHOUT HARDENING IT

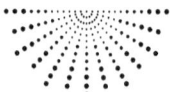

MONDAY DEVOTIONAL

There's a difference between guarding your heart and hardening it.

One is wisdom. The other is fear.

Proverbs 4:23 says:

> "Above all else, guard your heart, for everything you do flows from it" (NIV).

Guard your heart. Not harden it. Not lock it away. Not close it off completely.

Guard it.

That means you're protective, but not paralyzed. Careful, but not closed. Wise, but not walled off.

You've been hurt before. So you've built walls. High ones. Thick ones. Walls designed to keep pain out. And they work, pain can't get in.

But neither can love.

Because walls don't discriminate. They don't just keep out the bad, they keep out everything. And if you're not careful, you'll spend so much time protecting yourself that you'll miss out on the very thing you're longing for.

Guarding your heart means you're discerning. You pay attention to red flags. You don't ignore gut feelings. You don't rush into vulnerability with people who haven't earned it. You move at a healthy pace and protect what's sacred.

Hardening your heart means you've decided no one is trustworthy. You assume the worst. You sabotage good things before they can hurt you. You keep people at arm's length, not because they've done anything wrong, but because you're terrified they will.

One is protection. The other is prison.

And you've been living in a prison.

Jesus didn't guard His heart by refusing to love. He guarded it by loving wisely. He knew who to trust with what. He didn't pour Himself out to everyone equally, He was selective, intentional, discerning.

But He didn't harden His heart. Even knowing He'd be betrayed, rejected, and crucified, He still loved. Fully. Deeply. Sacrificially.

You can do the same.

You can be wise without being cynical. You can be careful without being closed off. You can protect yourself without shutting everyone out.

Guarding your heart doesn't mean refusing to be vulnerable. It means being intentional about who you're vulnerable with.

It means you don't hand your heart to just anyone. But when you meet someone who's proven trustworthy, someone who's shown up consistently, someone who's earned the right to see the real you, you don't withhold yourself out of fear.

You guard your heart. But you don't harden it.

Because a hardened heart might feel safer. But it's also lonelier.

And you weren't made for isolation. You were made for connection.

So lower the walls. Not all at once. Not recklessly. But intentionally, wisely, with people who've proven they're safe.

Guard your heart. But don't harden it.

MONDAY PRAYER

God, I've hardened my heart.

I've built walls so high that no one can get in. I've told myself it's wisdom, but it's really fear. I'm so terrified of being hurt again that I've shut everyone out.

And I don't want to live like this anymore.

Teach me the difference between guarding and hardening. Teach me how to be wise without being cynical. Teach me how to protect myself without isolating myself.

I don't want to hand my heart to just anyone. But I also don't want to withhold it from everyone. Help me find the balance.

Soften my heart without making me reckless. Make me discerning without making me distrustful. Help me guard wisely, not harden completely.

In Jesus' name, Amen.

TUESDAY PRAYER

Father, I'm afraid to be vulnerable again.

The last time I opened up, I got hurt. The last time I let someone in, they left. The last time I was honest about what I needed, I was told I was too much.

So I've decided it's safer to stay closed. To keep people at a distance. To never let anyone see the real me.

But that's not living. That's hiding.

Help me be brave enough to be vulnerable again. Not with everyone. Not recklessly. But with people who've earned it. People who've shown up. People who've proven they're safe.

I don't want fear to keep me from connection. I want wisdom to guide me toward healthy connection.

In Jesus' name, Amen.

WEDNESDAY PRAYER

Lord, I've been assuming the worst about everyone.

I meet someone new and immediately look for reasons not to trust them. I see potential and sabotage it before it can disappoint me. I expect people to hurt me because that's what I've experienced before.

But not everyone is like the people who hurt me. And assuming they are isn't wisdom, it's fear.

Help me stop punishing good people for bad people's mistakes. Help me give people a fair chance instead of writing them off before they've even started. Help me be discerning without being cynical.

Not everyone will hurt me. And I need to stop acting like they will.

In Jesus' name, Amen.

THURSDAY PRAYER

God, teach me how to guard my heart wisely.

I don't want to harden it. But I also don't want to be naïve. I don't want to hand my heart to people who haven't earned it, but I also don't want to withhold it from people who have.

Show me who's safe. Show me who's trustworthy. Show me who's proven themselves worthy of deeper access to my heart.

And give me the courage to lower the walls with those people. To be vulnerable. To let them in.

I want to guard wisely. Help me know the difference.

In Jesus' name, Amen.

FRIDAY PRAYER

Father, soften my heart.

I've been hard for so long that I don't know how to be soft anymore. I've protected myself so aggressively that I've lost the ability to be tender.

But I don't want to stay this way. I don't want to be so guarded that I can't experience real love. I don't want to be so afraid of pain that I miss out on connection.

Soften my heart. Not all at once. Not recklessly. But gently, carefully, intentionally.

Teach me to be strong and soft. Wise and open. Protected and present.

I don't want to harden my heart anymore. I want to guard it wisely and live fully.

In Jesus' name, Amen.

SATURDAY PRAYER

God, soften what I hardened in self-protection.

I built walls to keep pain out, and I kept everything else out too. This week, You showed me there's a better way, guard wisely, but don't close completely.

Give me discernment. Help me know who's earned access and who hasn't. Help me be brave enough to let the safe ones in.

In Jesus' name, Amen.

SUNDAY REFLECTION

Reflect:

- Have you been guarding your heart or hardening it? What's the difference in your life?

- Who has proven themselves safe enough to lower the walls with?

Declare:

- I will guard my heart without hardening it.

- I will be wise without being cynical.

- I will be open with people who've proven themselves trustworthy.

> **Carry This:** "Above all else, guard your heart, for everything you do flows from it.", Proverbs 4:23 (NIV)

SUNDAY PRAYER

God, soften what I hardened in self-protection.

I built walls to keep pain out and kept everything else out too. This week, You showed me there's a better way. Guard wisely, but don't close completely.

Give me discernment. Help me know who's earned access and who hasn't. Help me be brave enough to let the safe ones in.

In Jesus' name, Amen.

WEEK 20: HONORING YOUR BODY AS SACRED

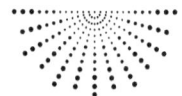

MONDAY DEVOTIONAL

Your body is not your own.

That's not meant to shame you. It's meant to elevate you.

1 Corinthians 6:19-20 says:

> "Do you not know that your bodies are temples of the Holy Spirit, who is in you, whom you have received from God? You are not your own; you were bought at a price. Therefore honor God with your bodies" (NIV).

Your body is a temple.

Not a tool for validation. Not a bargaining chip. Not something you give away casually to feel wanted, loved, or enough.

A temple. Sacred. Set apart. Worthy of honor.

And yet, the world has taught you the opposite. It's taught you that your body is currency. That if you want love, you have to give access. That if you want someone to stay, you have to compromise boundaries. That withholding yourself makes you uptight, old-fashioned, or undesirable.

But God's standard hasn't changed just because culture has.

Sexual purity isn't about God trying to keep good things from you. It's about God protecting something sacred for you.

Your body was designed for intimacy, real intimacy. The kind that happens in the safety of covenant, not the chaos of casual. The kind that's built on commitment, not convenience. The kind that honors, cherishes, and values, not uses, discards, and moves on.

And when you give your body outside of that context, it costs you something. Maybe not immediately. Maybe not visibly. But it costs you.

It costs you pieces of your heart. It costs you the ability to trust. It costs you the sacredness of what was meant to be holy. It costs you peace.

Because your body and your soul are connected. You can't separate them. And every time you give your body to someone who hasn't committed to your soul, you're tearing yourself apart.

God's not trying to punish you with boundaries. He's trying to protect you with them.

Now, maybe you've already crossed that line. Maybe you've already given your body in ways you wish you hadn't. Maybe you're carrying shame about past choices.

Hear this clearly: You are not disqualified.

God's grace covers that too. His mercy is bigger than your mistakes. And His forgiveness restores what you thought was permanently damaged.

But moving forward, you have a choice.

You can honor your body as sacred, or you can keep treating it as something to be used for validation, connection, or temporary comfort.

One leads to wholeness. The other leads to brokenness.

Your body is a temple. And it's time to start treating it that way.

MONDAY PRAYER

God, I haven't been honoring my body as sacred.

I've used it to feel wanted. I've compromised boundaries to keep people around. I've given it away casually, thinking it didn't matter, or hoping it would make someone love me.

But it did matter. And it cost me more than I realized.

Forgive me for not honoring what You've called sacred. Forgive me for treating my body like it was mine to use however I wanted, when You've called it a temple. Forgive me for giving access to people who hadn't earned it.

Teach me what it means to honor my body. Teach me that purity isn't about shame, it's about stewardship. Teach me that boundaries aren't restrictions, they're protection.

I want to honor You with my body. Help me make choices that reflect that.

In Jesus' name, Amen.

TUESDAY PRAYER

Father, I've believed the lie that my body is currency.

That if I want love, I have to give access. That if I want someone to stay, I have to compromise. That withholding myself makes me less desirable.

But that's not love. That's manipulation. And I don't want to build relationships on that foundation anymore.

Teach me what real love looks like. Teach me that someone who truly values me will honor my boundaries, not pressure me to cross them. Teach me that my worth isn't tied to my willingness to compromise.

I am not a transaction. I am a temple. And I'm choosing to honor that.

In Jesus' name, Amen.

WEDNESDAY PRAYER

Lord, I'm carrying shame about past choices.

I gave my body to people who didn't deserve it. I crossed lines I wish I hadn't. I compromised in ways that still haunt me.

And I'm afraid that I've disqualified myself. That I've damaged something that can't be restored.

But that's not true, is it? Your grace covers this too. Your mercy restores what was broken. Your forgiveness makes me clean again.

Help me receive that. Help me stop punishing myself for past mistakes. Help me believe that I can start honoring my body today, regardless of what I did yesterday.

I am not disqualified. I am redeemed. And I'm choosing to walk in that.

In Jesus' name, Amen.

THURSDAY PRAYER

God, give me the strength to hold boundaries.

I know what Your standard is. I know what honoring my body looks like. But when I'm lonely, when I'm tempted, when someone is pressuring me, it's hard to hold the line.

Give me strength when I'm weak. Give me clarity when I'm confused. Give me courage when I'm afraid of losing someone by saying no.

Remind me that anyone who can't respect my boundaries doesn't deserve access to my body. Remind me that real love honors, not pressures. Remind me that temporary loneliness is better than permanent regret.

Help me hold the line. Even when it's hard.

In Jesus' name, Amen.

FRIDAY PRAYER

Father, I want to honor You with my body.

Not out of obligation. Not out of fear. But because I believe You when You say it's sacred.

I believe that purity protects me. I believe that boundaries honor me. I believe that waiting is worth it, even when it's hard.

Help me live that out. Help me make choices that reflect what I believe. Help me honor my body as the temple You've called it to be.

I am sacred. And I'm choosing to live like it.

In Jesus' name, Amen.

SATURDAY PRAYER

God, I made commitments this week about how I'll treat my body.

Not out of shame. Not out of fear. But because I actually believe it's sacred.

The commitments will be tested. Temptation will come. I'll have weak moments.

But I wrote them down. I spoke them out loud. And when I'm tested, bring this moment back to my mind.

In Jesus' name, Amen.

SUNDAY REFLECTION

Reflect:

- How have you been treating your body, as sacred or as currency?

- What boundaries do you need to set to honor your body moving forward?

Declare:

- My body is a temple.

- I will honor it as sacred.

- I am worth protecting.

> **Carry This:** "Do you not know that your bodies are temples of the Holy Spirit, who is in you, whom you have received from God? You are not your own; you were bought at a price. Therefore honor God with your bodies.", 1 Corinthians 6:19-20 (NIV)

SUNDAY PRAYER

God, I made commitments this week about how I'll treat my body.

Not out of shame or fear, but because I believe it's sacred. The commitments will be tested. Temptation will come. I'll have weak moments.

But I wrote them down. I spoke them out loud. And when I'm tested, bring this moment back to my mind.

In Jesus' name, Amen.

WEEK 21: THE STRUGGLE WITH SEXUAL PURITY

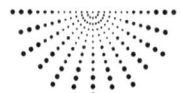

MONDAY DEVOTIONAL

Let's be honest about something the church often whispers about instead of addressing directly:

Sexual purity as a single adult is hard.

Not just hard, sometimes it feels impossible.

You have desires that are natural, God-given, and meant to be fulfilled in marriage. But you're not married. And depending on how long you've been single, you might be years, even decades, into waiting.

And the longer you wait, the harder it gets.

> The church tells you to "flee from sexual immorality" (1 Corinthians 6:18) but doesn't always give you practical tools for what that actually looks like when you're lonely, when you're tempted, when your body is screaming for something God says to wait for.

So let's talk about it honestly.

First: Your desire for sexual intimacy is not sinful. God created it. It's good, beautiful, and meant to bond you to another person in covenant.

The desire itself is not the problem, it's what you do with it that matters.

Second: Temptation is not sin. Jesus was tempted in every way, yet without sin (Hebrews 4:15). Being tempted doesn't make you dirty, weak, or less spiritual. It makes you human.

Third: Struggling doesn't mean failing. There's a difference between fighting and surrendering. If you're wrestling with this, if you're actively choosing purity even when it's hard, that's not failure. That's faithfulness.

But here's what you need to understand:

You cannot fight this battle on willpower alone.

You need practical strategies. You need accountability. You need to identify your triggers and avoid them. You need to fill your life with purpose, community, and intimacy (non-sexual) so you're not trying to meet every relational need through one avenue.

And most importantly, you need grace.

Because you're going to stumble. You're going to have moments where you compromise. You're going to fight this battle imperfectly.

And when that happens, the Enemy will tell you you've already failed, so you might as well keep going. He'll tell you you're too far gone, too broken, too addicted to ever change.

But that's a lie.

God's grace is bigger than your worst moment. His mercy is new every morning. And every single day, you get to choose again.

Sexual purity isn't about perfection. It's about direction. It's about getting back up every time you fall and choosing to honor God with your body again.

It's hard. No one's denying that.

But it's worth it. And you're not alone in the fight.

MONDAY PRAYER

God, this is hard.

I'm not going to pretend it's not. I'm not going to act like sexual purity is easy, because it's not. I have desires that are real, strong, and sometimes overwhelming. And the longer I wait, the harder it gets.

But I don't want to dishonor You with my body. I don't want to compromise what You've called sacred just because I'm tired of waiting.

Give me strength when I'm weak. Give me self-control when I'm tempted. Give me the courage to flee when I need to, even when every part of me wants to stay.

I can't do this on my own. I need You. Every single day.

In Jesus' name, Amen.

TUESDAY PRAYER

Father, I've stumbled.

I've compromised. I've crossed lines I said I wouldn't cross. And I'm ashamed.

But I'm not giving up. I'm not surrendering to the lie that I've already failed so I might as well keep going.

Forgive me. Cleanse me. Restore me. And give me the strength to choose differently tomorrow.

Your grace is bigger than my failure. Your mercy is new every morning. And I'm choosing to walk in that today.

In Jesus' name, Amen.

WEDNESDAY PRAYER

Lord, help me identify my triggers.

I know when I'm most vulnerable. I know what situations, what emotions, what circumstances make me more likely to compromise.

Give me the wisdom to avoid those triggers. Give me the courage to set boundaries, even when they feel extreme. Give me the strength to protect myself from situations where I know I'll struggle.

I can't fight this battle if I keep putting myself in the line of fire. Help me be smart about what I expose myself to.

In Jesus' name, Amen.

THURSDAY PRAYER

God, I need accountability.

I can't fight this alone. I need people who will ask the hard questions, who will check in, who will pray for me and with me.

Bring those people into my life. Give me the courage to be honest about my struggles instead of hiding them. Give me the humility to admit when I'm weak and ask for help.

This battle is too hard to fight alone. Help me find the support I need.

In Jesus' name, Amen.

FRIDAY PRAYER

Father, fill the void.

I know that sometimes sexual temptation is about more than just physical desire. Sometimes it's about loneliness. Sometimes it's about wanting to feel close to someone. Sometimes it's about trying to meet emotional needs in physical ways.

Help me identify what I'm really craving and meet that need in healthy ways. Fill the void with Your presence, with community, with purpose, so I'm not trying to fill it with something that will only leave me emptier.

I need You to satisfy what nothing else can.

In Jesus' name, Amen.

SATURDAY PRAYER

God, I was honest this week.

About how hard this is. About how much I'm struggling. About how badly I need Your help because willpower alone isn't cutting it.

I didn't fix everything. I didn't win every battle. But I asked for help. And that's something.

Tomorrow's another day. Another chance. Another fight. Be with me in it.

In Jesus' name, Amen.

SUNDAY REFLECTION

Reflect:

- What are your biggest triggers when it comes to sexual temptation?

- What practical strategies can you put in place to protect yourself?

Declare:

- I will honor God with my body.

- I will fight for purity, even when it's hard.

- God's grace is bigger than my struggle.

Carry This: "No temptation has overtaken you except what is common to mankind. And God is faithful; he will not let you be tempted beyond what you can bear. But when you are tempted, he will also provide a way out so that you can endure it.", 1 Corinthians 10:13 (NIV)

SUNDAY PRAYER

God, I was honest this week.

About how hard this is. About how much I'm struggling. About how badly I need Your help because willpower alone isn't cutting it.

I didn't fix everything. I didn't win every battle. But I asked for help. And that's something.

Tomorrow's another day. Another chance. Another fight. Be with me in it.

In Jesus' name, Amen.

WEEK 22: WHEN DESIRE FEELS LIKE A BURDEN

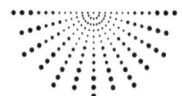

MONDAY DEVOTIONAL

Desire is supposed to be a gift.

But when you're single for longer than you planned, when you're waiting year after year with no end in sight, desire starts to feel like a burden.

It's the thing that wakes you up at 2 a.m., reminding you of what you don't have. It's the ache that shows up at weddings, when you're watching someone else promise forever. It's the longing that makes you feel like you're carrying a weight no one else understands.

And the worst part? You can't just turn it off.

You can't flip a switch and stop wanting companionship, intimacy, partnership. You can't pray it away, ignore it away, or willpower it away.

So what do you do when desire feels more like torment than gift?

First, you stop treating it like it's wrong.

God gave you the desire for relationship. He wired you for connection.

The longing you feel, for partnership, for intimacy, for someone to share life with, is not sinful. It's human.

Romans 8:23 says:

> "...we ourselves, who have the firstfruits of the Spirit, groan inwardly as we wait eagerly for our adoption to sonship, the redemption of our bodies" (NIV).

Even Paul acknowledged the groaning. The waiting. The tension between what is and what we're hoping for.

You're allowed to groan. You're allowed to ache. You're allowed to feel the weight of unfulfilled desire without shame.

But here's what you can't do: you can't let desire dictate your decisions.

When desire becomes a burden, it's easy to start making choices from a place of desperation instead of wisdom. You settle for less because you're tired of waiting for more. You compromise boundaries because the ache feels unbearable. You chase temporary relief instead of lasting fulfillment.

And that always costs you more than it gives.

So how do you carry desire well?

You acknowledge it. You bring it to God honestly. You don't pretend it doesn't exist or shame yourself for feeling it.

But you also don't let it control you. You don't make major decisions based on the intensity of the longing. You don't hand your heart over to someone just because they're willing to ease the ache temporarily.

You hold desire with open hands, honoring it as real, but refusing to let it become an idol.

And you trust that God sees it. That He's not ignoring your longing. That He's not cruel for giving you desires He hasn't fulfilled yet.

Desire is a burden some days. But it's also proof that you're alive, that you're capable of love, that you're made for more than isolation.

And one day, whether in this life or the next, every longing will be fulfilled.

Until then, you carry it. Honestly. Carefully. Hopefully.

MONDAY PRAYER

God, desire feels like a burden.

I didn't ask for this longing. I didn't choose to want partnership so deeply. But I do. And some days, it feels unbearable.

I'm tired of aching. I'm tired of waiting. I'm tired of feeling like I'm carrying a weight no one else understands.

But I don't want to shame myself for feeling this. I don't want to treat desire like it's sinful when You're the one who created it.

Help me carry it well. Help me acknowledge it without letting it control me. Help me honor it without making it an idol.

You see this longing. And I'm trusting that You're not ignoring it.

In Jesus' name, Amen.

TUESDAY PRAYER

Father, I'm tempted to settle.

The ache is so strong that I'm starting to think anything is better than nothing. I'm starting to look at people I know aren't right for me and wonder if I should compromise, just to ease the longing.

But I know that's not the answer. Settling won't satisfy the desire, it'll just create new pain.

Give me the strength to wait well. Give me the courage to hold out for what's healthy, even when the ache is screaming for relief. Give me the wisdom to know that temporary comfort isn't worth permanent regret.

I don't want to make decisions from desperation. I want to make decisions from wisdom.

In Jesus' name, Amen.

WEDNESDAY PRAYER

Lord, help me stop treating desire like it's the enemy.

I've been at war with my own longing. I've tried to ignore it, suppress it, shame it into submission. But it doesn't go away, it just goes underground and resurfaces when I'm most vulnerable.

Teach me to acknowledge desire without being controlled by it. Teach me that wanting companionship is not weak, needy, or unspiritual, it's human.

I don't need to fight against my own heart. I need to steward it well.

In Jesus' name, Amen.

THURSDAY PRAYER

God, I don't understand why You gave me desires You haven't fulfilled.

It feels cruel sometimes. Like You've wired me to want something and then withheld it indefinitely. And I don't know what to do with that.

But I'm choosing to trust You anyway. I'm choosing to believe that You're not ignoring my longing. That You see it, You care about it, and You have a plan, even when I can't see it.

Help me hold desire with open hands. Not clinging to it so tightly that it becomes an idol. Not rejecting it so completely that I harden my heart.

Just... holding it. Trusting You with it.

In Jesus' name, Amen.

FRIDAY PRAYER

Father, when desire feels unbearable, meet me there.

When the longing is so strong I can barely breathe, remind me that You're enough. Not in a cliché way. But in a real, tangible, "You see me and You're with me" way.

I'm not asking You to take the desire away. I'm just asking You to help me carry it. To give me strength when it feels like too much. To remind me that unfulfilled longing is not the same as abandoned hope.

You're with me in the ache. And that has to be enough for today.

In Jesus' name, Amen.

SATURDAY PRAYER

God, desire still aches.

You didn't take it away this week. I didn't expect You to. But You helped me carry it differently acknowledging it without letting it control me.

Some days the weight feels unbearable. Some days I'll resent it all over again.

But You're teaching me that unfulfilled longing isn't the same as unanswered prayer. You hear me. And that has to be enough.

In Jesus' name, Amen.

SUNDAY REFLECTION

Reflect:

- How has unfulfilled desire been affecting your decisions?

- What would it look like to carry desire well without letting it control you?

Declare:

- My desire for relationship is not sinful.

- I will not make decisions from desperation.

- I trust God with my unfulfilled longings.

> **Carry This:** "We ourselves, who have the firstfruits of the Spirit, groan inwardly as we wait eagerly for our adoption to sonship, the redemption of our bodies.", Romans 8:23 (NIV)

SUNDAY PRAYER

God, desire still aches.

You didn't take it away this week. I didn't expect You to. But You helped me carry it differently. Acknowledging it without letting it control me.

Some days the weight feels unbearable. Some days I'll resent it all over again. But You're teaching me that unfulfilled longing isn't the same as unanswered prayer.

You hear me. And that has to be enough.

In Jesus' name, Amen.

WEEK 23: HEALING FROM TOXIC RELATIONSHIPS

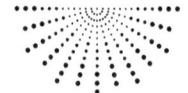

MONDAY DEVOTIONAL

Some relationships don't just end badly, they leave damage.

You walked away, but pieces of you stayed behind. The way they made you feel about yourself. The things they said that you can't unhear. The patterns they created that you can't seem to break.

And even though you're out, you're still carrying the toxicity with you.

Maybe it was the one who made you feel like you were never enough. Who moved the goalposts every time you got close. Who praised you one day and tore you down the next, keeping you off-balance and desperate for their approval.

Maybe it was the one who isolated you from everyone who cared about you. Who made you doubt your own reality. Who convinced you that you were the problem, always.

Maybe it was the one who used your vulnerabilities against you. Who knew exactly where you were weakest and exploited it.

Toxic relationships rewire how you see yourself. They teach you that love is conditional, unstable, dangerous. They make you believe that you have to earn affection, that you're only valuable when you're useful, that your needs are too much.

And those lessons don't disappear just because the relationship did.

Psalm 34:18 says:

> "The Lord is close to the brokenhearted and saves those who are crushed in spirit" (NIV).

God sees the damage. He sees what that relationship cost you. And He's close to you in it.

Healing from a toxic relationship means more than just moving on. It means actively unlearning what they taught you about love, about yourself, about what you deserve.

It means identifying the lies they planted and replacing them with truth. It means recognizing the patterns they created and choosing different ones. It means giving yourself permission to grieve what happened without minimizing it.

You might catch yourself making excuses for them. Remembering the good moments and questioning whether it was really that bad. Wondering if you're being dramatic.

You're not.

If you felt small, afraid, or constantly on edge, that was real. If you lost yourself trying to keep them happy, that mattered. If you're still dealing with the aftermath, that's valid.

Healing takes time. You're going to have moments where you slip back into old patterns. Where you hear their voice in your head. Where you question your own worth the way they taught you to.

But every time you catch it, every time you counter the lie with truth, every time you choose differently, you're healing.

God is close to you in this. Closer than you realize.

And He's going to restore what was broken.

MONDAY PRAYER

God, that relationship left damage I'm still carrying.

The way they made me feel about myself. The things they said that replay in my head. The patterns they created that I can't seem to shake.

I thought leaving would be enough, but I'm still dealing with the aftermath. I'm still undoing the damage. I'm still trying to remember who I was before they convinced me I was someone else.

Help me heal. Help me unlearn the lies they taught me. Help me see myself the way You see me, separate from how they made me feel.

I know You're close to the brokenhearted. So be close to me now. Heal what they broke. Restore what they damaged.

I'm ready to be whole again.

In Jesus' name, Amen.

TUESDAY PRAYER

Father, I keep making excuses for them.

I remember the good moments and forget how bad it really was. I downplay what happened because some days it feels easier than facing how much it hurt.

But minimizing the damage doesn't help me heal. It just keeps me stuck.

Give me clarity. Help me see the relationship for what it actually was, toxic, damaging, unhealthy. Help me stop romanticizing the past and face the truth about what I endured.

I deserve to acknowledge the full reality of what happened. And I deserve to heal from it.

In Jesus' name, Amen.

WEDNESDAY PRAYER

Lord, I'm still hearing their voice.

The criticism. The doubt. The way they made me question my own reality. It's like they're still in my head, even though they're gone from my life.

Silence their voice. Replace it with Yours. Remind me that their opinion of me was wrong. That their treatment of me was unjust. That I am not who they said I was.

I don't want to carry their words anymore. I want to hear Your truth instead.

In Jesus' name, Amen.

THURSDAY PRAYER

God, help me recognize the patterns they created.

I see myself doing things I learned in that relationship. Shrinking myself. Over-explaining. Apologizing for things that aren't my fault. Walking on eggshells around people who haven't earned that level of caution.

Those patterns served me then, they kept me safe in an unsafe situation. But they're hurting me now.

Help me identify them. Help me see when I'm operating from old trauma instead of present reality. Help me choose different responses.

I'm not in that relationship anymore. I don't need those survival mechanisms.

In Jesus' name, Amen.

FRIDAY PRAYER

Father, I'm grieving what I lost.

Not just the relationship. But the version of myself I was before it. The confidence I had. The trust I gave freely. The belief that I deserved to be treated well.

That relationship took things from me that I'm not sure I'll ever fully get back.

But I'm asking You to restore what was stolen. To rebuild what was broken. To give me back the parts of myself I thought were gone forever.

You are close to the brokenhearted. So be close to me. And heal me.

In Jesus' name, Amen.

SATURDAY PRAYER

God, I named what happened.

I stopped minimizing. Stopped making excuses. Stopped pretending it wasn't that bad.

It was that bad. And acknowledging it is the first step toward actually healing from it.

The damage is still there. The patterns are still showing up. But I'm not ignoring them anymore.

And that's progress.

In Jesus' name, Amen.

SUNDAY REFLECTION

Reflect:

- What lies did that toxic relationship teach you about yourself?

- What patterns from that relationship are you still carrying?

Declare:

- Toxic relationships leave damage that takes time to heal.

- I will not minimize what happened to make it easier to carry.

- God is close to the brokenhearted, and He's restoring me. God is restoring what was broken.

> **Carry This: "The Lord is close to the brokenhearted and saves those who are crushed in spirit.", Psalm 34:18 (NIV)**

SUNDAY PRAYER

God, I named what happened this week.

I stopped minimizing, stopped making excuses, stopped pretending it wasn't that bad. It was that bad. And acknowledging it is the first step toward actually healing from it.

The damage is still there. The patterns are still showing up. But I'm not ignoring them anymore. And that's progress.

In Jesus' name, Amen.

WEEK 24: LETTING GO OF WHAT COULD HAVE BEEN

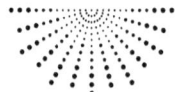

MONDAY DEVOTIONAL

You're still holding onto a version of the relationship that never existed.

The version where they finally saw your worth. Where they changed. Where everything you invested actually paid off. Where it all worked out the way you hoped.

But that version only exists in your head.

And as long as you keep holding onto it, you can't fully move forward.

Letting go of what actually happened is hard enough. But letting go of what could have been? That's brutal.

Because what could have been feels so close. If they had just chosen differently. If you had just done something differently. If the timing had been better. If circumstances had aligned.

You replay the relationship looking for the moment where it could have turned around. You imagine alternate endings where everything works out. You fantasize about them realizing what they lost and coming back changed.

And every time you do, you're keeping the wound open.

> Ecclesiastes 3:6 says there's "a time to search and a time to give up, a time to keep and a time to throw away" (NIV).

There's a time to let go.

You've searched. You've analyzed. You've replayed it a thousand times. And you still don't have the ending you wanted.

Because that ending was never available. You couldn't have loved them into wholeness. You couldn't have fixed what they weren't willing to fix. You couldn't have made it work alone.

The relationship you're grieving, the one where they loved you well, where they met you halfway, where it all worked out, that relationship never existed. You're mourning a fantasy.

And I know that sounds harsh. But staying tethered to what could have been is keeping you from seeing what actually is, and what could actually be.

You can't move forward while you're still facing backward. You can't receive what's coming if your hands are full of what never was.

Let it go. All of it. The person you thought they were. The relationship you thought you had. The future you imagined together.

Let go of the fantasy so you can make room for reality.

MONDAY PRAYER

God, I'm still holding onto what could have been.

I keep replaying the relationship, looking for the moment where it could have worked. I keep imagining a version where they changed, where I was enough, where it all worked out.

But that version never existed. And holding onto it is keeping me stuck.

Help me let go. Help me release the fantasy so I can face reality. Help me stop grieving a relationship that only lived in my head.

I can't move forward while I'm still holding onto what never was.

In Jesus' name, Amen.

TUESDAY PRAYER

Father, I keep imagining they'll come back different.

That one day they'll realize what they lost. That they'll do the work. That they'll become the person I always hoped they'd be.

But waiting for that keeps me tethered to someone who's already moved on. It keeps me stuck in hope that's really just denial.

Help me stop waiting for a version of them that may never exist. Help me accept who they actually are and let go of who I wanted them to be.

I deserve to move forward. And I can't do that while I'm still waiting for them to change.

In Jesus' name, Amen.

WEDNESDAY PRAYER

Lord, I'm mourning a future that was never real.

I had plans. I had hopes. I could see the life we'd build together. And even though the relationship ended, I'm still grieving the future I lost.

But that future was never guaranteed. And holding onto it is keeping me from the future You actually have for me.

Help me release what I thought was coming. Help me trust that You have something better, something real, something healthy, something that doesn't require me to bend myself into someone else.

I'm letting go of what could have been so I can receive what actually will be.

In Jesus' name, Amen.

THURSDAY PRAYER

God, help me stop replaying the relationship.

I keep going back, analyzing every moment, looking for where it went wrong. Wondering if I had just said something different, done something different, been different, maybe it would have worked.

But I can't change the past. And torturing myself with "what ifs" isn't helping me heal.

Give me the strength to stop replaying. To stop analyzing. To stop searching for answers that won't change the outcome.

It ended. And I need to make peace with that.

In Jesus' name, Amen.

FRIDAY PRAYER

Father, I'm releasing what never was.

The relationship I thought I had. The person I thought they were. The future I thought we'd have together.

All of it, I'm letting it go.

I can't carry it anymore. And I can't move forward while I'm still holding onto it.

Help me release it fully. Help me make peace with what actually happened instead of staying attached to what I wished had happened.

I'm ready to let go.

In Jesus' name, Amen.

SATURDAY PRAYER

God, I released the fantasy.

The version of the relationship that only existed in my head. The future I imagined that was never actually available.

My hands feel empty now. But they're also open.

Open to receive what's real instead of clinging to what never was. Fill them with something better.

In Jesus' name, Amen.

SUNDAY REFLECTION

Reflect:

- What version of the relationship are you still holding onto that never actually existed?

- What would it look like to fully let go of what could have been?

Declare:

- Letting go of what could have been makes room for what actually will be.

- The relationship I'm grieving only existed in my imagination.

- I'm releasing the fantasy so I can embrace reality.

> **Carry This:** "There is a time for everything, and a season for every activity under the heavens: ...a time to search and a time to give up, a time to keep and a time to throw away.", Ecclesiastes 3:1, 6 (NIV)

SUNDAY PRAYER

God, I released the fantasy this week.

The version of the relationship that only existed in my head. The future I imagined that was never actually available. My hands feel empty now.

But they're also open. Open to receive what's real instead of clinging to what never was. Fill them with something better.

In Jesus' name, Amen.

WEEK 25: WHEN YOU KEEP CHOOSING THE WRONG PERSON

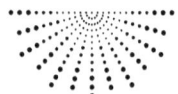

MONDAY DEVOTIONAL

You know the feeling.

You meet someone new, and within the first conversation, something pulls you in. There's chemistry. Intensity. A spark.

And somewhere in the back of your mind, a quiet voice says, "This feels familiar."

You ignore it. You tell yourself this time is different. This person is different.

But six months later, you're sitting in the same wreckage, wondering how you ended up here again.

Same dynamic. Same ending. Different person.

You keep choosing the same type. And you need to figure out why before you do it again.

Let's get specific. Who do you keep choosing?

The Fixer-Upper. They have so much potential. They're almost perfect, they just need a little help. A little support. Someone who believes in them. And you're convinced that if you love them well enough, they'll finally become who they could be. But they never do. Because you can't fix someone who isn't willing to do the work themselves.

The Emotionally Unavailable One. They're charming. They're interesting. But they're always just out of reach. They text just enough to keep you hooked but never enough to make you feel secure. They show up when it's convenient but disappear when you need them. And you tell yourself they'll open up eventually, but they won't. Because they don't want to.

The Chaos Creator. The relationship is a rollercoaster. High highs. Low lows. Intense passion followed by intense conflict. You confuse the drama for depth, the intensity for intimacy. And you stay because calm feels boring compared to the adrenaline rush of chaos. But chaos isn't love. It's just chaos.

The One Who Keeps You Guessing. You never know where you stand. One day they're all in. The next day they're pulling back. They keep you off-balance, chasing reassurance, trying to prove you're worth choosing. And you mistake the uncertainty for excitement. But it's not excitement. It's anxiety.

Here's what all of these have in common: they keep you focused on them instead of on yourself.

When you're trying to fix someone, you're not dealing with your own wounds. When you're chasing someone emotionally unavailable, you're not facing your fear of real intimacy. When you're addicted to chaos, you're not learning what healthy stability feels like.

You keep choosing these people because something in you believes this is what you deserve. Or because this is what love looked like growing up. Or because you're trying to rewrite an old story with a new person.

But until you heal what's driving the pattern, you'll keep repeating it.

Proverbs 4:23 says,

> "Above all else, guard your heart, for everything you do flows from it" (NIV).

Everything flows from your heart. Including who you choose.

So what's in your heart that keeps pulling you toward the wrong person?

Figure that out. Heal it. And then choose differently.

MONDAY PRAYER

God, I see the pattern now.

I keep choosing the same type of person, just with a different name. The Fixer-Upper. The Emotionally Unavailable One. The Chaos Creator. The one who keeps me guessing.

And I'm tired of it.

Show me what's in my heart that keeps pulling me toward these people. What wound am I trying to heal? What need am I trying to meet? What lie am I believing about what I deserve?

Heal it. Uproot it. Replace it with truth.

I don't want to do this again. Help me break the cycle.

In Jesus' name, Amen.

TUESDAY PRAYER

Father, I've been choosing people I can fix.

Because when I'm focused on their brokenness, I don't have to deal with mine. When I'm working on them, I feel needed. Valuable. Like I have a purpose.

But that's not love. That's codependency.

Teach me that I don't have to fix anyone to be valuable. That my worth isn't tied to whether I can save someone. That choosing someone who's already doing the work is actually healthier than choosing someone who needs me to do it for them.

I want a partner, not a project.

In Jesus' name, Amen.

WEDNESDAY PRAYER

Lord, I'm drawn to people who are emotionally unavailable.

And I've told myself a hundred different reasons why. They're busy. They're guarded. They just need time.

But the truth is, I'm afraid of real intimacy. Chasing someone who won't fully let me in means I never have to fully show up either.

Heal my fear of being truly known. Heal whatever makes me settle for breadcrumbs instead of holding out for someone who's actually available.

I deserve someone who shows up. Help me believe that.

In Jesus' name, Amen.

THURSDAY PRAYER

God, I've confused chaos with chemistry.

I thought the drama meant we were passionate. I thought the rollercoaster meant we were alive. I thought if it didn't feel intense, it wasn't real.

But I was wrong. Intensity isn't intimacy. Drama isn't depth. And chaos isn't love.

Rewire my understanding. Teach me what healthy love actually feels like. Show me that steady doesn't mean boring. That peace doesn't mean passionless.

I don't need chaos. I need consistency.

In Jesus' name, Amen.

FRIDAY PRAYER

Father, I'm walking away this time.

I see the signs. I recognize the type. I know where this leads.

And I'm choosing differently.

It feels wrong. Everything in me wants to stay, wants to give them a chance, wants to believe it'll be different this time.

But I know better. And I'm trusting what I know over what I feel.

Give me strength to follow through. To not go back. To hold the line even when I'm lonely.

I'm breaking the pattern. And I'm not looking back.

In Jesus' name, Amen.

SATURDAY PRAYER

God, breaking patterns is terrifying.

Everything familiar feels safe, even when it's destructive. Everything different feels wrong, even when it's healthy.

But I made a decision this week, I'm done repeating the same mistakes. I'm choosing differently, even when it scares me.

Hold me to it. When I'm tempted to go back to what I know, remind me why I'm walking away.

In Jesus' name, Amen.

SUNDAY REFLECTION

Reflect:

- Which type do you keep choosing? The Fixer-Upper? The Emotionally Unavailable One? The Chaos Creator? The One Who Keeps You Guessing?

- What wound or belief is driving you toward that type?

Declare:

- I've been choosing the same person because I believed that's what I deserved.

- Breaking the pattern requires healing the belief driving it.

- Healthy love might feel unfamiliar, but that doesn't make it wrong.

> **Carry This:** "Above all else, guard your heart, for everything you do flows from it.", Proverbs 4:23 (NIV)

SUNDAY PRAYER

God, breaking patterns is terrifying.

Everything familiar feels safe, even when it's destructive. Everything different feels wrong, even when it's healthy. But I made a decision this week. I'm done repeating the same mistakes.

Hold me to it. When I'm tempted to go back to what I know, remind me why I'm walking away.

In Jesus' name, Amen.

WEEK 26: BECOMING WHOLE, NOT JUST LOOKING FOR COMPLETION

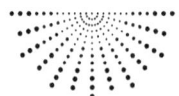

MONDAY DEVOTIONAL

There's a difference between wanting a relationship and needing one to feel complete.

One is a healthy desire. The other is desperation.

And if you're honest, you've crossed that line more times than you want to admit.

You've looked at your life and thought, "Once I meet someone, then I'll be happy. Then my life will make sense. Then I'll finally feel whole."

And you've made decisions from that place, staying in relationships that weren't right because being with someone felt better than being alone. Compromising standards because you were afraid you'd never find anyone better. Ignoring red flags because you needed to believe this was finally it.

But here's what you're learning: no person can complete you.

They can complement you. They can walk beside you. They can add richness to an already full life.

But they can't fill a void that only God can fill.

Philippians 4:19 says,

> "And my God will meet all your needs according to the riches of his glory in Christ Jesus" (NIV).

All your needs. Every single one. The loneliness. The longing for companionship. The desire to be known and loved.

God meets those needs. Sometimes through people. Sometimes directly. Sometimes in ways you don't expect.

But always through Him.

When you enter a relationship from a place of wholeness, everything changes. You're choosing to share your life with someone, you're inviting them into something that's already full, already meaningful, already purposeful.

When you enter from a place of lack, you're asking them to be your life. To give you meaning. To make you whole.

And that's a weight no human was designed to carry.

So what does it mean to become whole?

It means your identity is secure in Christ, whether you're single or not. It means you have purpose, community, and joy that exist independent of your relationship status. It means you're living fully right now, building a life worth sharing, with or without someone else.

Wholeness doesn't mean you stop wanting a relationship. It means your life isn't on hold until you have one.

You're complete. Today. Right now. In Christ.

And when the right person comes, if they come, they won't complete you.

They'll walk beside someone who's already whole.

MONDAY PRAYER

God, I've been looking for someone to complete me.

I've made relationships the answer to everything I'm missing. I've put pressure on people to fill voids they were never meant to fill.

And it's never worked. Because what I was really looking for could only be found in You.

Forgive me for looking to people to do what only You can do. Forgive me for making relationships an idol. Forgive me for believing the lie that I'm incomplete without someone.

Teach me what it means to be whole in You. Teach me that my life has meaning right now. Teach me to build something worth sharing instead of waiting for someone to give me a life worth living.

I am complete in You. Help me believe that.

In Jesus' name, Amen.

TUESDAY PRAYER

Father, I don't want to enter my next relationship from a place of desperation.

I want to enter it from a place of wholeness. I want to invite someone into a life that's already full instead of asking them to be my life.

But I don't know how to get there. I don't know what it looks like to be whole while still longing for companionship.

Show me. Teach me. Help me build a life that's meaningful right now, with purpose, community, joy, so that when someone comes, I'm ready. Truly ready.

I want to be whole first. Help me get there.

In Jesus' name, Amen.

WEDNESDAY PRAYER

Lord, I've been putting my life on hold.

Waiting until I meet someone to pursue dreams. Waiting until I'm in a relationship to feel like my life really matters. Waiting for someone else to give me permission to live fully.

But that's a waste. And I don't want to do it anymore.

Help me build a life worth living right now. Help me pursue purpose, invest in community, chase dreams, all of it. Help me stop treating singleness like a waiting room and start living like this season matters.

I am whole. And my life has meaning today.

In Jesus' name, Amen.

THURSDAY PRAYER

God, help me stop measuring my worth by whether someone chooses me.

I've tied my value to my relationship status for too long. I've believed that being chosen by someone proves I'm worthy. That being loved by a person validates my existence.

But my worth comes from You. My value was settled at the cross. And whether someone chooses me or doesn't choose me doesn't change that.

Help me anchor my identity in You. Help me know, deeply, fully, that I am valuable because I'm Yours.

I don't need someone to complete me. I'm already complete in You.

In Jesus' name, Amen.

FRIDAY PRAYER

Father, I'm becoming whole.

I'm building a life that matters. I'm pursuing purpose. I'm investing in community. I'm finding joy that doesn't depend on my relationship status.

And I'm doing it because You're teaching me that wholeness comes from You, from living fully in this season, whatever it looks like.

Help me keep going. Help me keep building. Help me keep believing that I'm complete in You, whether I'm single or not.

I am whole. And I'm living like it.

In Jesus' name, Amen.

SATURDAY PRAYER

God, I'm building something.

A life that matters. A life that's full. A life worth sharing with someone instead of asking someone to be my life.

I'm still learning what wholeness looks like. Still figuring out how to live fully while still longing for partnership.

But I'm doing it. And for the first time in a long time, I actually believe my life has meaning right now, with or without someone beside me.

In Jesus' name, Amen.

SUNDAY REFLECTION

Reflect:

- Have you been looking for someone to complete you or to complement you?

- What would it look like to build a life worth sharing instead of waiting for someone to give you a life?

Declare:

- I am whole in Christ.

- I am building a life worth living right now.

- I don't need someone to complete me.

> **Carry This: "And my God will meet all your needs according to the riches of his glory in Christ Jesus.", Philippians 4:19 (NIV)**

SUNDAY PRAYER

God, I'm building something.

A life that matters. A life that's full. A life worth sharing with someone instead of asking someone to be my life. I'm still learning what wholeness looks like.

But I'm doing it. And for the first time in a long time, I actually believe my life has meaning right now. With or without someone beside me.

In Jesus' name, Amen.

WEEK 27: YOU WERE MADE FOR MORE THAN MARRIAGE

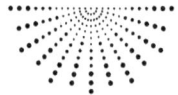

MONDAY DEVOTIONAL

Marriage is good. But it's not your purpose.

Let that sink in for a second, because the church has done a terrible job of making this clear.

We celebrate engagements like they're the pinnacle of spiritual achievement. We treat marriage like it's the ultimate goal, the thing that validates your existence, the finish line you're racing toward.

And we leave singles feeling like their lives are on pause until they cross it.

But here's what Scripture actually says:

> You were created in the image of God (Genesis 1:27). You were saved to do good works that God prepared in advance for you (Ephesians 2:10). You were called to make disciples (Matthew 28:19). You were given spiritual gifts to build up the body of Christ (1 Corinthians 12).

Notice what's missing from that list? Marriage.

Marriage is a gift. It's a good gift. But it's not the reason you exist.

You have a calling that's bigger than your relationship status. You have purpose that exists whether you're single or married. You have work to do in the kingdom that doesn't require a ring on your finger.

And if you spend your entire single season waiting for marriage to give your life meaning, you're wasting the calling God has already given you.

Paul addressed this directly in 1 Corinthians 7. He talks about the advantages of singleness, the freedom to serve God without divided attention, the ability to focus fully on kingdom work, the flexibility to go where married people can't go.

He wasn't saying marriage is bad. He was saying singleness has unique value that shouldn't be dismissed.

But somewhere along the way, the church forgot that. And now we have generations of singles who believe their lives don't really start until they say "I do."

That's a lie. And it's costing you years you'll never get back.

God gave you gifts for a reason. He placed you in this season for a reason. He has work for you to do right now, work that matters, work that builds His kingdom, work that won't wait until you're married.

Marriage might be part of your story. But it's not the whole story.

You were made for more.

MONDAY PRAYER

God, I've made marriage my purpose.

I've treated it like the finish line, the validation, the thing that makes my life matter. And I've put everything else on hold waiting for it.

Forgive me for making a gift into an idol. Forgive me for treating marriage like it's the reason I exist when You've already given me purpose that has nothing to do with my relationship status.

Open my eyes to what You've actually called me to do. Show me the work You've prepared for me. Remind me that I was made for more than just finding someone.

I have a calling. Help me step into it instead of waiting for permission.

In Jesus' name, Amen.

TUESDAY PRAYER

Father, I've been living like my life doesn't start until I'm married.

I've put dreams on hold. I've delayed purpose. I've treated this season like a waiting room instead of a season with its own calling.

But You didn't put my purpose on pause. You've been calling me to something this whole time, and I've been too distracted to hear it.

What do You want me to do right now? What work have You prepared for me in this season? What gifts have You given me that I'm supposed to be using?

Show me. And give me the courage to pursue it, whether I'm single or not.

In Jesus' name, Amen.

WEDNESDAY PRAYER

Lord, I've bought into the lie that marriage is the ultimate goal.

That once I'm married, my life will finally make sense. That finding someone is more important than finding my calling.

But that's backward. And it's keeping me from the work You've given me to do.

Reorder my priorities. Help me see that building Your kingdom matters more than building my own comfort. That making disciples is more important than making plans for a wedding. That using my gifts right now is more valuable than waiting for the "right time."

I was made for more than marriage. Help me live like I believe that.

In Jesus' name, Amen.

THURSDAY PRAYER

God, show me what I'm called to do in this season.

Not what I'll do when I'm married. Not what I'll do when my life is "settled." What You're calling me to do right now.

Give me clarity. Give me direction. Give me the courage to step into purpose even when it feels uncertain.

I don't want to waste this season waiting. I want to use it. I want to invest it in work that matters, work that builds Your kingdom, work that I won't be able to do the same way if my circumstances change.

You've given me this time. Help me steward it well.

In Jesus' name, Amen.

FRIDAY PRAYER

Father, I want to live with kingdom priorities.

I want to care more about advancing Your purposes than advancing my own timeline. I want to invest in what matters eternally instead of obsessing over what matters temporarily.

Give me Your perspective. Help me see my life the way You see it, as someone with a calling, with purpose, with work to do that's bigger than my relationship status.

I was made for more than marriage. And I'm choosing to live like it.

In Jesus' name, Amen.

SATURDAY PRAYER

God, You shifted something this week.

You reminded me that my life has meaning right now. That I have a calling that exists whether I ever get married or not. That You've prepared work for me to do, and it's time to stop waiting and start doing it.

I don't have it all figured out yet. I don't know exactly what it looks like. But I know I'm done putting my purpose on hold.

Give me courage to step into what You're calling me to. Even if it scares me. Even if it's not what I planned.

In Jesus' name, Amen.

SUNDAY REFLECTION

Reflect:

- Have you been treating marriage as your ultimate purpose? What dreams have you put on hold waiting for it?

- What might God be calling you to do in this season that you've been ignoring?

Declare:

- Marriage is a gift, but it's not my purpose.

- I have a calling that exists right now.

- I was made for more than finding someone.

> **Carry This:** "For we are God's handiwork, created in Christ Jesus to do good works, which God prepared in advance for us to do.",
> **Ephesians 2:10 (NIV)**

SUNDAY PRAYER

God, You shifted something this week.

You reminded me that my life has meaning right now. That I have a calling that exists whether I ever get married or not. That You've prepared work for me to do.

I don't have it all figured out yet. But I know I'm done putting my purpose on hold. Give me courage to step into what You're calling me to.

In Jesus' name, Amen.

WEEK 29: STEWARDSHIP OF YOUR SINGLE SEASON

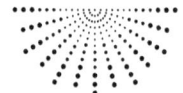

MONDAY DEVOTIONAL

This season is a gift. And like every gift, you're responsible for how you use it.

You didn't ask for it. You might not want it. But you have it.

And God is going to ask you what you did with it.

Jesus told a parable in Matthew 25 about a master who gave his servants different amounts of money and then left. When he returned, he asked each one to give an account of what they'd done with what they'd been given.

Two of them invested it and multiplied it. One buried it in the ground out of fear.

The master praised the two who stewarded well. And he condemned the one who wasted what he'd been given.

Your single season is what you've been given. And one day, God is going to ask you what you did with it.

Did you invest it or bury it? Did you steward it well or waste it wishing it was something else?

Stewardship means you're intentional with what you have. You don't squander it. You don't coast through it on autopilot. You recognize that every season has value, and you treat it accordingly.

So what does good stewardship of your single season look like?

It means you're investing in relationships that matter, deepening friendships, serving your community, building connections that will outlast this season.

It means you're pursuing purpose, using your gifts, discovering your calling, doing work that builds the kingdom.

It means you're growing spiritually, developing disciplines, dealing with wounds, becoming the person God's calling you to be.

It means you're managing your resources wisely, your time, your money, your energy. You're not just killing time until something changes. You're investing it in things that matter.

And here's the hard part: good stewardship means you stop treating this season like a punishment and start treating it like an opportunity.

Because it is.

You have freedom right now that you won't have later. You have time. You have flexibility. You have resources that aren't divided.

Use them. Steward them well. Don't bury them in the ground because you're angry you didn't get what you wanted.

God gave you this season. And He's going to ask what you did with it.

Make sure you have an answer.

MONDAY PRAYER

God, I haven't been stewarding this season well.

I've been coasting. Complaining. Wasting time wishing things were different instead of investing in what's actually here.

Forgive me for burying what You gave me. Forgive me for treating this season like something to survive instead of something to steward.

Show me how to invest this time well. Show me what You want me to do with the freedom, the resources, the opportunities I have right now.

I don't want to waste this. Help me steward it faithfully.

In Jesus' name, Amen.

TUESDAY PRAYER

Father, I've been treating this season like it doesn't count.

Like it's just filler until my real life starts. Like nothing I do right now actually matters because I'm single.

But that's a lie. This season counts. Every day of it.

Help me stop wasting it. Help me invest in what matters, relationships, purpose, growth. Help me treat this time like the gift it is instead of the punishment I've made it out to be.

You gave me this season. And I'm going to steward it well.

In Jesus' name, Amen.

WEDNESDAY PRAYER

Lord, show me where I'm wasting time.

Where am I coasting when I should be investing? Where am I distracting myself when I should be engaging? Where am I squandering resources You've given me?

Bring it to light. I can't steward well if I'm not honest about where I'm failing.

Give me the courage to make changes. To stop wasting time on things that don't matter and start investing in things that do.

In Jesus' name, Amen.

THURSDAY PRAYER

God, I want to steward my relationships well.

I've been so focused on finding "the one" that I've neglected the people already in my life. I've put friendships on the back burner. I've withdrawn from community.

But those relationships matter. And they're part of what You've given me to steward in this season.

Help me invest in them. Help me show up, engage, build connections that will last beyond my single years.

I don't want to look back and realize I wasted this season being lonely when I was surrounded by people who cared.

In Jesus' name, Amen.

FRIDAY PRAYER

Father, teach me to steward my resources well.

My time. My money. My energy. My gifts.

I have freedom right now that I won't always have. I have flexibility. I have opportunities.

Show me how to use them wisely. Show me where to invest, where to serve, where to give. Show me how to make the most of what I've been given.

This season is a gift. And I'm choosing to treat it like one.

In Jesus' name, Amen.

SATURDAY PRAYER

God, I made changes this week.

I stopped coasting. I started investing. I made decisions about how I'm going to steward this season instead of just letting it pass me by.

This is just the beginning. But it's a start.

Help me follow through. Help me stay intentional. Help me keep stewarding well, even when it's hard, even when I'm tired, even when I'd rather just coast.

You gave me this season. And I'm not wasting it.

In Jesus' name, Amen.

SUNDAY REFLECTION

Reflect:

- If God asked you today what you've done with your single season, what would you say?

- What's one area where you need to steward better, relationships, purpose, growth, or resources?

Declare:

- This season is a gift I'm responsible for stewarding.

- I will invest, not bury, what God has given me.

- I will make the most of the freedom and opportunities I have right now.

> **Carry This:** "His master replied, 'Well done, good and faithful servant! You have been faithful with a few things; I will put you in charge of many things. Come and share your master's happiness!'" , Matthew 25:21 (NIV)

SUNDAY PRAYER

God, I made changes this week.

I stopped coasting. I started investing. I made decisions about how I'm going to steward this season instead of just letting it pass me by. This is just the beginning.

Help me follow through. Help me stay intentional. Help me keep stewarding well, even when it's hard.

You gave me this season. And I'm not wasting it.

In Jesus' name, Amen.

WEEK 30: BUILDING KINGDOM COMMUNITY

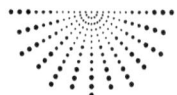

MONDAY DEVOTIONAL

You were never meant to do life alone.

Even in your singleness, especially in your singleness, you need community.

Real community. The kind that shows up when things fall apart. The kind that knows your struggles and doesn't run. The kind that prays with you, challenges you, celebrates with you.

But somewhere along the way, you stopped investing in it.

Maybe you got tired of being the only single person in your friend group. Maybe you pulled back because you didn't want to be a burden. Maybe you convinced yourself you'd invest in community once you were married.

But here's the reality: isolation is killing you.

And it's not what God designed.

Ecclesiastes 4:9-10 says,

> "Two are better than one, because they have a good return for their labor: If either of them falls down, one can help the other up. But pity anyone who falls and has no one to help them up" (NIV).

You need people. And people need you.

Community isn't a nice-to-have. It's essential. It's how the body of Christ functions. It's how you grow, how you heal, how you survive the hard seasons.

And you can't wait until you're married to build it.

So what does kingdom community look like?

It's more than showing up to church on Sunday. It's more than small talk in the lobby. It's deeper than surface-level friendships that never get past "How are you?"

Kingdom community is people who know your story. Who ask hard questions. Who call you out when you're off track. Who show up when you're struggling, even when it's inconvenient.

It's people you serve with, pray with, do life with. It's relationships that go beyond your comfort zone, that challenge you to grow, that remind you you're not alone.

And here's what you need to hear: building that kind of community requires effort.

You have to initiate. You have to be vulnerable. You have to invest time, energy, and consistency into relationships that matter.

It won't happen by accident. And it won't happen if you're waiting for someone to pursue you first.

You need community. So stop waiting for it to come to you.

Go build it.

MONDAY PRAYER

God, I've isolated myself.

I've pulled back from community because it felt easier than showing up. I've convinced myself I don't need people the way I actually do.

But isolation is destroying me. And it's not what You designed.

Give me courage to re-engage. To reach out. To be vulnerable with people even when it's scary. To invest in relationships that go deeper than small talk.

I need community. And I'm ready to do the work to build it.

In Jesus' name, Amen.

TUESDAY PRAYER

Father, I've been waiting for community to come to me.

I've expected people to pursue me, to notice I'm struggling, to invite me in. And when they didn't, I took it as proof that I don't belong.

But that's not how it works. Building community requires effort. And I haven't been putting in the work.

Give me the courage to initiate. To reach out first. To be the one who invites, who follows up, who shows up consistently.

I can't wait for community to find me. I have to go build it.

In Jesus' name, Amen.

WEDNESDAY PRAYER

Lord, help me find my people.

I need relationships that go deeper than surface level. I need people who actually know me, who I can be honest with, who will walk through hard things with me.

Lead me to them. Open my eyes to the people You've already placed around me. Give me wisdom to know who's safe, who's trustworthy, who's worth investing in.

And give me the courage to be vulnerable. To let people in. To stop protecting myself so fiercely that no one can actually reach me.

I need community. Show me where to find it.

In Jesus' name, Amen.

THURSDAY PRAYER

God, I've been a terrible friend.

I've been so consumed with my own stuff, my own loneliness, my own struggles, my own desires, that I haven't shown up for the people around me.

Forgive me for that. Forgive me for only thinking about what I need from community instead of what I can give to it.

Help me be the kind of friend I want to have. Help me show up. Help me serve. Help me invest in others the way I want them to invest in me.

Community is give and take. And I've been taking without giving back.

In Jesus' name, Amen.

FRIDAY PRAYER

Father, I want to build something that lasts.

I want relationships that go beyond this season. I want community that will still be there when my circumstances change. I want friendships that matter, that go deep, that actually reflect the body of Christ.

Give me patience. Give me consistency. Give me the willingness to invest even when it's hard, even when it's inconvenient, even when I don't feel like it.

Kingdom community is worth the effort. And I'm ready to build it.

In Jesus' name, Amen.

SATURDAY PRAYER

God, I took steps this week.

I reached out. I showed up. I initiated instead of waiting for someone else to pursue me.

It's just the beginning. Building real community takes time. But I'm committed to the process.

Help me stay consistent. Help me keep showing up, keep investing, keep being vulnerable even when it's uncomfortable.

I need community. And I'm building it.

In Jesus' name, Amen.

SUNDAY REFLECTION

Reflect:

- Have you been isolating yourself? What's one step you can take this week to re-engage with community?

- Who are the people God has already placed around you that you could invest in more deeply?

Declare:

- I was not meant to do life alone.

- Building community requires effort, and I'm willing to do the work.

- I will initiate, invest, and show up consistently.

Carry This: "Two are better than one, because they have a good return for their labor: If either of them falls down, one can help the other up.", Ecclesiastes 4:9-10a (NIV)

SUNDAY PRAYER

God, I took steps this week.

I reached out. I showed up. I initiated instead of waiting for someone else to pursue me. It's just the beginning. Building real community takes time.

But I'm committed to the process. Help me stay consistent. Help me keep showing up, keep investing, keep being vulnerable.

I need community. And I'm building it.

In Jesus' name, Amen.

WEEK 31: SERVING FROM OVERFLOW, NOT EMPTINESS

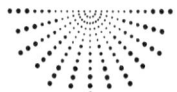

MONDAY DEVOTIONAL

You can't pour from an empty cup.

You've heard that before. And you've probably ignored it.

Because when you're single, people expect you to serve. You have the time, right? You have the flexibility. You don't have a spouse or kids demanding your attention.

So you say yes. To everything. To everyone.

You serve at church. You help friends move. You're the one everyone calls when they need something. You show up, you give, you pour out.

And eventually, you run dry.

Because you've been serving from emptiness instead of overflow.

There's a difference.

Serving from overflow means you're full first. You've spent time with God. You've rested. You've filled your own tank so that what you give to others comes from abundance, not depletion.

Serving from emptiness means you're running on fumes. You're giving what you don't have. You're saying yes when you should say no because you feel guilty, obligated, or afraid of disappointing people.

And eventually, that leads to burnout, bitterness, and resentment.

Jesus modeled this perfectly. He served constantly. He healed, taught, and poured Himself out for people. But He also withdrew. He pulled away to pray. He rested. He said no to demands so He could stay connected to the Father.

> Luke 5:15-16 says, "Yet the news about him spread all the more, so that crowds of people came to hear him and to be healed of their sicknesses. But Jesus often withdrew to lonely places and prayed" (NIV).

But Jesus often withdrew.

He didn't serve nonstop. He knew He couldn't give to others what He wasn't receiving from the Father.

And you can't either.

Serving is good. Generosity is good. Using your gifts to bless others is good.

But if you're doing it from a place of emptiness, it's not sustainable. And it's not healthy.

You need to fill your own cup first. You need to spend time with God, rest your body, nurture your soul. You need to say no sometimes so you can say yes from a place of strength instead of obligation.

Serving from overflow doesn't mean you're selfish. It means you're wise.

And it means the service you give actually lasts.

MONDAY PRAYER

God, I've been serving from emptiness.

I've said yes to everything because I thought that's what I was supposed to do. I've poured myself out until there's nothing left. And now I'm running on fumes.

Forgive me for neglecting my own soul while trying to serve everyone else. Forgive me for believing that saying no makes me selfish. Forgive me for ignoring the warning signs that I was burning out.

Teach me to serve from overflow. Teach me that filling my own cup first isn't selfish. It's necessary. Teach me that I can't give what I don't have.

Help me rest. Help me pull away. Help me say no when I need to.

In Jesus' name, Amen.

TUESDAY PRAYER

Father, I'm exhausted.

I've been giving and giving and giving until there's nothing left. And I don't know how to stop.

I feel guilty saying no. I feel selfish prioritizing my own rest. I feel like if I'm not constantly serving, I'm failing.

But that's not true, is it? You didn't design me to run on empty. You didn't call me to burn out for the sake of other people's approval.

Give me permission to rest. Give me courage to say no. Give me wisdom to know when I'm serving from overflow and when I'm just depleting myself.

I can't keep doing this. Something has to change.

In Jesus' name, Amen.

WEDNESDAY PRAYER

Lord, teach me the difference between generosity and depletion.

I want to be generous. I want to serve. I want to use my gifts to bless others.

But I've crossed the line into depletion. I've given so much that I have nothing left for myself, nothing left for You.

Show me where the line is. Show me how to serve from a place of strength instead of exhaustion. Show me how to fill my own cup so that what I give comes from abundance.

Generosity is good. But depletion isn't sustainable.

In Jesus' name, Amen.

THURSDAY PRAYER

God, I need to withdraw.

I need to pull away from the noise, the demands, the constant requests for my time and energy. I need to spend time with You without distraction.

But I feel guilty about it. Like I'm abandoning people who need me. Like I'm being selfish.

Remind me that even Jesus withdrew. That rest isn't optional. That I can't serve well if I'm running on empty.

Give me the courage to say no. Give me the strength to protect my time with You. Give me the wisdom to know when to engage and when to pull back.

I need to withdraw so I can serve from overflow.

In Jesus' name, Amen.

FRIDAY PRAYER

Father, I'm setting boundaries.

I'm saying no to things I used to say yes to. I'm protecting my time, my energy, my capacity to actually rest and be filled.

And it feels uncomfortable. People might be disappointed. They might not understand.

But I can't keep serving from emptiness. And I'm choosing health over approval.

Give me strength to hold these boundaries. Give me confidence that saying no isn't selfish. Give me peace when people push back.

I'm serving from overflow now. And that means I have to fill my cup first.

In Jesus' name, Amen.

SATURDAY PRAYER

God, I rested this week.

I pulled away. I said no. I spent time filling my own cup instead of constantly pouring out.

And it felt strange. Uncomfortable. Like I was doing something wrong.

But I wasn't. I was doing what You modeled. I was withdrawing so I could serve from a place of strength instead of depletion.

Help me keep this rhythm. Help me serve from overflow instead of emptiness. Help me remember that rest isn't selfish. It's necessary.

In Jesus' name, Amen.

SUNDAY REFLECTION

Reflect:

- Are you serving from overflow or from emptiness? How can you tell the difference?

- What do you need to say no to so you can fill your own cup first?

Declare:

- I cannot pour from an empty cup.

- Serving from overflow is wise, not selfish.

- Rest is necessary, not optional.

> Carry This: "Yet the news about him spread all the more, so that crowds of people came to hear him and to be healed of their sicknesses. But Jesus often withdrew to lonely places and prayed.", Luke 5:15-16 (NIV)

SUNDAY PRAYER

God, I rested this week.

I pulled away. I said no. I spent time filling my own cup instead of constantly pouring out. And it felt strange, uncomfortable, like I was doing something wrong.

But I wasn't. I was doing what You modeled. Help me keep this rhythm. Help me serve from overflow instead of emptiness.

In Jesus' name, Amen.

WEEK 33: BEING PRESENT WHERE GOD HAS YOU

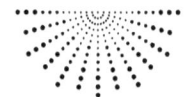

MONDAY DEVOTIONAL

You're always somewhere else.

Physically, you're here. But mentally, you're five years in the future, imagining a life that doesn't exist yet.

You're planning for a relationship you don't have. You're decorating a home you haven't bought. You're picturing a family you haven't started.

And while you're busy living in the future, you're missing the present.

God has you here, right now, for a reason. And if you spend this entire season wishing you were somewhere else, you're going to miss what He's doing in this one.

Psalm 31:15 says,

> "My times are in your hands" (NIV).

Your times. Not just your future. Your present. The season you're in right now.

God has you here. In this job. In this city. In this church. In this stage of life. And He didn't put you here by accident.

But you're not present enough to see what He's doing.

You're too busy resenting where you are. Too focused on where you wish you were. Too distracted by the life you think you're supposed to have to notice the life you actually have.

And you're missing it.

Being present doesn't mean you stop hoping for the future. It doesn't mean you stop praying for change. It doesn't mean you pretend you don't want more.

It means you stop living five years ahead and start living right here, right now.

It means you notice the people around you. You engage with the opportunities in front of you. You steward the season you're actually in instead of the one you're waiting for.

It means you ask, "God, what are You doing here? What do You want me to see? Who do You want me to serve? What am I supposed to learn in this moment?"

Because if you're always somewhere else, you'll never fully be anywhere.

Stop waiting for your life to start. It already has.

Be present.

MONDAY PRAYER

God, I'm never fully here.

Physically, I'm present. But mentally, I'm always somewhere else. Always in the future. Always imagining a life that doesn't exist yet.

And I'm missing what's actually happening right now.

Forgive me for wasting this season by refusing to be in it. Forgive me for being so focused on what's coming that I can't see what's here.

Teach me to be present. Teach me to notice what You're doing right now. Teach me to engage with the people, the opportunities, the moments You've placed in front of me.

My times are in Your hands. Help me trust that where I am right now is exactly where I need to be.

In Jesus' name, Amen.

TUESDAY PRAYER

Father, I keep missing what's in front of me.

I'm so distracted by what I don't have that I can't appreciate what I do have. I'm so focused on the future that I'm blind to the present.

And I know I'm missing it. I know there are people, opportunities, and moments I'm letting slip by because I'm not paying attention.

Open my eyes. Help me see what You're doing right now. Help me notice the people You've placed in my path. Help me be fully present in the life I actually have instead of the one I'm waiting for.

I don't want to waste this season. Help me be here.

In Jesus' name, Amen.

WEDNESDAY PRAYER

Lord, what are You doing here?

I've been so busy resenting where I am that I haven't stopped to ask what You're doing in it.

What are You trying to show me? Who are You calling me to serve? What am I supposed to learn in this season?

I'm listening. I'm paying attention. I'm here.

Show me what I've been missing.

In Jesus' name, Amen.

THURSDAY PRAYER

God, help me stop rushing.

I rush through conversations because I'm thinking about the next thing. I rush through moments because I'm focused on where I'm going instead of where I am.

But life isn't happening in the future. It's happening right now.

Slow me down. Help me be fully present in conversations. Help me engage with people instead of just getting through interactions. Help me notice the moments I usually miss because I'm too distracted to see them.

I don't want to rush through my life. Help me be here.

In Jesus' name, Amen.

FRIDAY PRAYER

Father, I trust that You have me here for a reason.

I don't fully understand it yet. I don't see the full picture. But I believe You didn't put me here by accident.

So I'm choosing to be present. I'm choosing to engage. I'm choosing to stop wishing I was somewhere else and start living fully where I am.

Show me what You're doing. I'm ready to see it.

In Jesus' name, Amen.

SATURDAY PRAYER

God, I was present this week.

I stopped living five years in the future and started living right here, right now. I noticed things I usually miss. I engaged with people I usually overlook. I saw what You're doing that I've been too distracted to see.

And it changed things. Being present made this season feel less like a burden and more like an opportunity.

Help me stay here. Help me keep noticing, keep engaging, keep being fully in the life I actually have.

In Jesus' name, Amen.

SUNDAY REFLECTION

Reflect:

- Are you present in your life, or are you always somewhere else mentally?

- What's one thing God might be doing right now that you've been too distracted to notice?

Declare:

- My times are in God's hands.

- I will be present where He has me.

- I will stop living in the future and start living right now.

> **Carry This: "Therefore do not worry about tomorrow, for tomorrow will worry about itself. Each day has enough trouble of its own.", Matthew 6:34 (NIV)**

SUNDAY PRAYER

God, I was present this week.

I stopped living five years in the future and started living right here, right now. I noticed things I usually miss. I engaged with people I usually overlook.

And it changed things. Being present made this season feel less like a burden and more like an opportunity. Help me stay here.

In Jesus' name, Amen.

WEEK 34: WHEN YOUR PURPOSE FEELS UNCLEAR

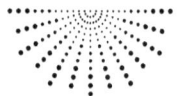

MONDAY DEVOTIONAL

You want a clear, detailed map of your purpose. God wants you to trust Him one step at a time.

And that's frustrating.

You pray for clarity. You ask for direction. You beg God to just show you the plan so you can move forward with confidence.

And the answer is usually just the next step. Not the whole journey. Just one step.

Proverbs 3:5-6 says,

> "Trust in the Lord with all your heart and lean not on your own understanding; in all your ways submit to him, and he will make your paths straight" (NIV).

Notice it doesn't say He'll give you a detailed roadmap. It says He'll make your paths straight. As you go. As you trust. As you submit.

You don't get the whole plan upfront. You get the next step.

And that requires faith.

Maybe your purpose feels unclear because you're waiting for total clarity before you move. Maybe you're paralyzed by the fear of getting it wrong. Maybe you think God owes you a blueprint before you commit.

But that's not how faith works.

Faith moves without seeing the whole staircase. Faith takes the next step without knowing where step ten leads. Faith trusts that God is guiding even when the path isn't clear.

So what do you do when your purpose feels unclear?

You stop waiting for perfect clarity and start moving in the direction that seems right. You pay attention to open doors and closed ones. You try things, experiment, see where God leads.

You ask, "God, what's the next step?" instead of "God, show me the whole plan."

And you trust that He'll give you what you need, when you need it.

Purpose isn't always revealed in a single moment. Sometimes it unfolds over years. And clarity comes as you move, not before you start.

So take the next step. Even if you don't know where step five leads.

God will meet you there.

MONDAY PRAYER

God, I want the whole plan.

I want to know where I'm going, what I'm supposed to be doing, how it's all going to work out. But You're only giving me the next step.

And that's hard for me.

Teach me to trust You without seeing the whole picture. Teach me to move without needing perfect clarity. Teach me that faith means taking the next step even when I can't see the tenth one.

Show me the next step. And give me the courage to take it.

In Jesus' name, Amen.

TUESDAY PRAYER

Father, I'm afraid of getting it wrong.

What if I take a step and it's the wrong one? What if I invest time in something that's not actually my purpose? What if I miss what You're calling me to because I moved too soon?

But waiting in fear isn't better than moving and course-correcting.

Give me confidence to try. To experiment. To step out in faith, trusting that You'll redirect me if I'm headed the wrong way.

I'd rather move and adjust than stay frozen in fear.

In Jesus' name, Amen.

WEDNESDAY PRAYER

Lord, what's the next step?

Not the whole plan. Not the ten-year vision. Just the next step.

What door are You opening? What opportunity are You placing in front of me? What burden are You placing on my heart that I need to act on?

Show me. And I'll move.

In Jesus' name, Amen.

THURSDAY PRAYER

God, help me pay attention.

To open doors. To closed ones. To where You're leading and where You're blocking.

I've been so focused on forcing clarity that I haven't been paying attention to what You're already showing me.

Open my eyes. Help me see where You're moving. Help me notice the path You're making straight.

In Jesus' name, Amen.

FRIDAY PRAYER

Father, I'm taking the next step.

I don't know where it leads. I don't have the whole plan. But I know this is the right next move.

So I'm doing it. And I'm trusting that You'll show me step two when I get there.

Give me faith to keep moving, one step at a time.

In Jesus' name, Amen.

SATURDAY PRAYER

God, I moved this week without having all the answers.

And it felt uncomfortable. Uncertain. Like I was stepping out onto unstable ground.

But You met me there. You showed me the next step. And I'm learning that clarity comes as I move, not before.

Help me keep trusting You with the journey, even when I can't see the destination.

In Jesus' name, Amen.

SUNDAY REFLECTION

Reflect:

- Have you been waiting for perfect clarity before you move? What's one step you could take right now?

- Where might God already be showing you the next step that you've been ignoring?

Declare:

- I don't need the whole plan to take the next step.

- God will make my paths straight as I trust Him.

- Clarity comes through movement, not before it.

> **Carry This: "Trust in the Lord with all your heart and lean not on your own understanding; in all your ways submit to him, and he will make your paths straight.", Proverbs 3:5-6 (NIV)**

SUNDAY PRAYER

God, I'm learning to trust You without seeing the whole plan.

It's hard. I want clarity. I want certainty. But You're teaching me that faith means moving anyway.

This week, I took a step without knowing where it leads. And that's progress. Help me keep going. Keep showing me the next step. I'm trusting You with the rest.

In Jesus' name, Amen.

WEEK 35: LIVING FULLY, NOT HALF-ALIVE

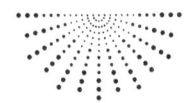

MONDAY DEVOTIONAL

You've been surviving. It's time to start living.

There's a difference. And you know it.

Surviving means you wake up, go through the motions, check the boxes, and go to bed. You're functioning. You're getting by. But you're not actually alive.

Living fully means you're engaged. You're pursuing things that matter. You're investing in relationships, dreams, purpose. You're feeling deeply, risking boldly, showing up completely.

And somewhere along the way, you stopped doing that.

Maybe it was self-protection. Maybe you convinced yourself that if you don't get your hopes up, you won't get hurt. Maybe you've been living at half capacity because full capacity felt too vulnerable.

But that's not the life Jesus offered.

John 10:10 says,

> "The thief comes only to steal and kill and destroy; I have come that they may have life, and have it to the full" (NIV).

Life to the full.

Not survival mode. Not coasting. Not just getting by until something changes.

Full life. Abundant life. Life that's rich, deep, meaningful, purposeful.

And you can have that right now. Today. Whether you're single or not.

Living fully doesn't mean you have to be happy all the time. It doesn't mean life is easy or pain-free. It doesn't mean pretending everything is fine when it's not.

It means you're present. You're engaged. You're feeling your emotions instead of numbing them. You're taking risks instead of playing it safe. You're pursuing what matters instead of waiting for permission.

It means you stop putting life on hold until circumstances change. You stop telling yourself you'll really start living when you meet someone, when you get the job, when things finally work out.

You start now.

What would it look like to live fully in the season you're actually in?

It might mean pursuing a dream you've been putting off. It might mean deepening friendships you've been neglecting. It might mean taking a risk you've been avoiding. It might mean feeling the grief you've been suppressing.

Whatever it is, it requires you to stop surviving and start living.

You were made for more than just getting by.

MONDAY PRAYER

God, I've been surviving, not living.

Going through the motions. Checking boxes. Getting by. But I'm not actually alive. I'm numb. I'm disengaged. I'm coasting.

And I don't want to do that anymore.

Wake me up. Stir something in me. Remind me what it feels like to be fully alive, fully engaged, fully present.

You came to give me abundant life. Help me actually live it instead of just surviving until something changes.

In Jesus' name, Amen.

TUESDAY PRAYER

Father, I've been protecting myself by staying half-alive.

If I don't get my hopes up, I won't get hurt. If I don't invest fully, I won't be disappointed. If I stay numb, I won't feel the pain.

But that's not living. That's just slow death.

Give me courage to feel again. To hope again. To risk again. To engage fully even when it's scary.

I'd rather be hurt while living than safe while surviving.

In Jesus' name, Amen.

WEDNESDAY PRAYER

Lord, what have I put on hold?

What dreams have I shelved? What risks have I avoided? What parts of myself have I shut down because I've been waiting for the "right time"?

Bring them back to the surface. Remind me what it feels like to pursue something that matters. Remind me what I'm capable of when I'm actually engaged.

I'm done waiting. I'm ready to live.

In Jesus' name, Amen.

THURSDAY PRAYER

God, help me stop numbing.

I've been numbing the pain, the loneliness, the disappointment. But in the process, I've numbed everything else too. I can't feel joy because I've shut down feeling altogether.

Teach me to feel again. The good and the bad. The joy and the grief. The hope and the disappointment.

I want to be alive again. Fully alive.

In Jesus' name, Amen.

FRIDAY PRAYER

Father, I'm choosing to live fully today.

Not waiting for circumstances to change. Not waiting for permission. Not waiting until I feel ready.

Today, I'm engaging. I'm pursuing. I'm showing up completely. I'm living the life I have instead of the one I'm waiting for.

Give me strength to keep choosing this. To keep living fully even when it's hard.

In Jesus' name, Amen.

SATURDAY PRAYER

God, I felt alive this week.

I stopped surviving and started living. I took risks. I pursued something that mattered. I let myself feel instead of staying numb.

And it reminded me what I've been missing. What I've been avoiding. What's possible when I actually engage.

Help me keep living this way. Help me resist the urge to go back to survival mode. Help me stay fully alive.

In Jesus' name, Amen.

SUNDAY REFLECTION

Reflect:

- Have you been surviving or living? What's the difference in your life?

- What would it look like to live fully in the season you're actually in?

Declare:

- I was made for abundant life, not survival mode.

- I will stop waiting for circumstances to change before I start living.

- I am choosing to live fully, right now.

> **Carry This:** "The thief comes only to steal and kill and destroy; I have come that they may have life, and have it to the full.", John 10:10 (NIV)

SUNDAY PRAYER

God, You came to give me abundant life.

And this week, I got a taste of what that actually means. Not just surviving, but living. Fully. Deeply. Completely.

I don't want to go back to coasting. I don't want to numb out again. I want to stay here, in this place of being fully alive.

Help me keep choosing life. Every single day.

In Jesus' name, Amen.

WEEK 36: THE FREEDOM TO SAY YES

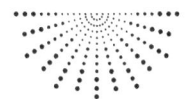

MONDAY DEVOTIONAL

Singleness gives you a freedom married people don't have.

The freedom to say yes.

Yes to opportunities that require flexibility. Yes to risks that require availability. Yes to callings that require undivided attention.

Married people have responsibilities. They have to consider another person's schedule, another person's needs, another person's dreams. They can't just pick up and move. They can't say yes to every opportunity that comes along.

But you can.

And if you're not careful, you'll waste this freedom wishing it away instead of using it.

Paul understood this. In 1 Corinthians 7:32-34, he talks about the freedom of singleness. The ability to focus on the Lord's affairs without distraction. The opportunity to serve in ways that require complete devotion.

He wasn't saying marriage is bad. He was saying singleness has unique advantages. And one of the biggest is freedom.

So what are you doing with it?

Are you saying yes to opportunities God places in front of you? Are you taking risks you couldn't take if your life looked different? Are you using this season to do things you won't be able to do later?

Or are you so focused on what you don't have that you're missing what you do have?

Freedom to travel. Freedom to relocate. Freedom to take a job that doesn't pay well but aligns with your calling. Freedom to invest time in ministry, service, or creative pursuits without negotiating with anyone else.

You have options right now that you might not have later.

Use them.

Say yes to the mission trip you've been putting off. Say yes to the career change that scares you. Say yes to the move, the risk, the opportunity that requires everything you have.

You have the freedom to say yes. And that freedom is a gift.

Don't waste it waiting for the season when you'll have less of it.

MONDAY PRAYER

God, I have freedom I've been ignoring.

Freedom to say yes to opportunities, to take risks, to pursue things that require flexibility. But I've been so focused on what I don't have that I haven't noticed what I do have.

Open my eyes. Show me the opportunities You're placing in front of me. Show me where I can say yes in ways I won't be able to later.

I have freedom right now. Help me use it wisely.

In Jesus' name, Amen.

TUESDAY PRAYER

Father, what are You calling me to say yes to?

What opportunity have You placed in front of me that I've been ignoring? What risk requires the freedom I have right now? What door are You opening that I need to walk through?

Show me. And give me courage to say yes.

In Jesus' name, Amen.

WEDNESDAY PRAYER

Lord, I've been playing it safe.

Staying comfortable. Avoiding risk. Turning down opportunities because they felt too uncertain, too demanding, too hard.

But what if those opportunities were gifts? What if You were giving me chances to do things I won't be able to do later?

Forgive me for wasting the freedom You've given me. Give me courage to stop playing it safe and start saying yes.

In Jesus' name, Amen.

THURSDAY PRAYER

God, help me stop resenting the freedom I have.

I've been so focused on wanting the responsibilities of marriage that I've missed the opportunities of singleness. I've been envying what I don't have instead of stewarding what I do.

Shift my perspective. Help me see freedom as a gift, not a burden. Help me use it instead of resenting it.

In Jesus' name, Amen.

FRIDAY PRAYER

Father, I'm saying yes.

To the opportunity You've placed in front of me. To the risk that requires everything I have. To the calling that demands the freedom I have right now.

It's scary. It's uncertain. But I know this is what You're asking me to do.

Give me courage to follow through. To step out. To use the freedom I've been given.

In Jesus' name, Amen.

SATURDAY PRAYER

God, I said yes this week.

To something I couldn't have done if my life looked different. To an opportunity that required the freedom I have right now.

And it felt good. It reminded me that singleness isn't just something to endure. It's a season with unique opportunities.

Help me keep saying yes. Help me keep using the freedom You've given me while I still have it.

In Jesus' name, Amen.

SUNDAY REFLECTION

Reflect:

- What opportunities have you turned down because they required freedom you were taking for granted?

- What's one thing you could say yes to right now that you might not be able to say yes to later?

Declare:

- I have freedom that married people don't have.

- I will use this freedom to say yes to what God is calling me to.

- This season offers opportunities I won't always have.

> **Carry This:** "An unmarried man is concerned about the Lord's affairs, how he can please the Lord. But a married man is concerned about the affairs of this world, how he can please his wife, and his interests are divided.", 1 Corinthians 7:32-34a (NIV)

SUNDAY PRAYER

God, freedom is a gift I've been taking for granted.

This week, You showed me opportunities I've been ignoring. Risks I could take. Chances to say yes in ways I won't always be able to.

I don't want to waste this season wishing I had different responsibilities. I want to use the freedom I actually have.

Help me say yes boldly. Help me steward this gift well.

In Jesus' name, Amen.

WEEK 37: THE COURAGE TO PURSUE DREAMS NOW

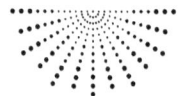

MONDAY DEVOTIONAL

You've been waiting for permission to pursue your dreams.

Permission from circumstances. Permission from other people. Permission from some future version of yourself that's more qualified, more prepared, more ready.

But that permission isn't coming.

You either pursue your dreams now, or you keep waiting for a "better time" that may never arrive.

Ecclesiastes 11:4 says,

> "Whoever watches the wind will not plant; whoever looks at the clouds will not reap" (NIV).

If you wait for perfect conditions, you'll never start.

The dream you've been carrying? The business you want to start? The book you want to write? The mission you want to pursue? The skill you want to develop?

You keep telling yourself you'll do it later. When you're married. When you have more time. When you feel more confident. When circumstances align.

But later never comes.

Because there will always be a reason to wait. There will always be something that's not quite right. There will always be uncertainty, risk, or fear.

So you have a choice. You can keep waiting for perfect conditions, or you can start now with what you have.

Dreams don't require perfect circumstances. They require courage.

Courage to start before you're ready. Courage to risk failure. Courage to invest time and energy in something that might not work out.

And you have that courage. You just haven't been using it.

So what's the dream you've been putting off?

What would it look like to take one step toward it today? Not the whole journey. Just one step.

You don't need permission. You don't need perfect conditions. You don't need someone to validate your calling.

You just need to start.

MONDAY PRAYER

God, I've been waiting for permission to pursue my dreams.

Permission from circumstances. Permission from other people. Permission from some future version of myself that has it all together.

But that permission isn't coming. And I'm realizing that if I don't start now, I might never start.

Give me courage to pursue what You've placed on my heart. Give me boldness to take the first step even when I'm not ready. Give me faith to believe that You'll provide what I need as I go.

I'm done waiting. I'm starting now.

In Jesus' name, Amen.

TUESDAY PRAYER

Father, I've been using my singleness as an excuse.

"I'll do it when I'm married." "I'll have more time later." "I'll be more qualified then."

But those are just excuses. And they're keeping me from doing what You've called me to do.

Forgive me for wasting time waiting for better conditions. Forgive me for treating my dreams like they're optional. Forgive me for burying what You've given me.

I'm done making excuses. Show me the first step, and I'll take it.

In Jesus' name, Amen.

WEDNESDAY PRAYER

Lord, I'm afraid of failure.

What if I pursue this dream and it doesn't work out? What if I invest time and energy and end up with nothing to show for it? What if I'm not as capable as I thought?

But fear of failure is keeping me from even trying. And that's worse than failing.

Give me courage to risk. To try. To step out even when success isn't guaranteed.

I'd rather fail while pursuing something that matters than succeed at playing it safe.

In Jesus' name, Amen.

THURSDAY PRAYER

God, what's the first step?

I've been overwhelmed by the size of the dream. It feels too big, too complicated, too far out of reach.

But I don't need to do it all at once. I just need to take the first step.

Show me what that is. And give me courage to take it today.

In Jesus' name, Amen.

FRIDAY PRAYER

Father, I'm taking action.

I'm not waiting for perfect conditions. I'm not waiting for someone to give me permission. I'm not waiting until I feel ready.

I'm starting now. With what I have. Where I am.

Give me strength to keep going. Give me perseverance when it gets hard. Give me faith to believe You'll provide what I need as I move forward.

In Jesus' name, Amen.

SATURDAY PRAYER

God, I started this week.

I took a step toward the dream I've been carrying. It wasn't perfect. It wasn't huge. But it was something.

And it reminded me that I'm capable of more than I've been doing. That the dream is possible. That You're with me in the pursuit.

Help me keep going. Help me take the next step. And the one after that.

In Jesus' name, Amen.

SUNDAY REFLECTION

Reflect:

- What dream have you been putting off waiting for "better conditions"?

- What's one specific step you could take this week toward that dream?

Declare:

- I don't need permission to pursue my dreams.

- Perfect conditions will never come, so I'm starting now.

- I have the courage to take the first step.

> **Carry This: "Whoever watches the wind will not plant; whoever looks at the clouds will not reap.", Ecclesiastes 11:4 (NIV)**

SUNDAY PRAYER

God, I'm pursuing what You've placed on my heart.

Not waiting for perfect conditions. Not waiting for permission. Just starting. With courage. With faith. With what I have.

This week, I took a step I've been avoiding for too long. And it felt good. It felt right. It felt like I was finally doing what I was made for.

Help me keep going. Keep showing me the next step. Keep giving me courage to pursue this dream.

In Jesus' name, Amen.

WEEK 38: YOU DON'T NEED PERMISSION TO THRIVE

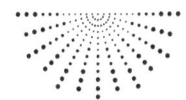

MONDAY DEVOTIONAL

You've been waiting for someone to give you permission to thrive.

Permission to be happy while you're single. Permission to enjoy your life before you're married. Permission to build something meaningful even though your life doesn't look the way you thought it would.

But that permission isn't coming from anyone else.

You have to give it to yourself.

Somewhere along the way, you internalized the message that you're not allowed to fully thrive until certain conditions are met. Until you're in a relationship. Until you've "arrived" at whatever milestone you think validates your life.

And you've been living in that limbo ever since. Half-engaged. Half-alive. Waiting for circumstances to change before you allow yourself to be happy.

But here's the truth: God isn't waiting for your circumstances to change before He gives you permission to thrive.

He's already given it.

Psalm 16:11 says,

> "You make known to me the path of life; you fill me with joy in your presence, with eternal pleasures at your right hand" (NIV).

Joy in His presence. Not joy when you're married. Not joy when life looks the way you want. Joy in His presence, right now.

You don't need to wait for permission to be happy. You don't need to apologize for enjoying your life while you're single. You don't need to feel guilty for thriving in a season that doesn't match your expectations.

You're allowed to be joyful. You're allowed to build a life you love. You're allowed to thrive, right now, exactly as you are.

So what would that look like?

Maybe it means finally decorating your space the way you want instead of treating it like temporary housing. Maybe it means pursuing hobbies you've been putting off. Maybe it means traveling, investing in friendships, or building something meaningful.

Whatever it is, you don't need to wait for someone to validate it.

You have permission. From God. From yourself.

Now give yourself the freedom to actually use it.

MONDAY PRAYER

God, I've been waiting for permission to thrive.

Permission to be happy. Permission to enjoy my life. Permission to build something meaningful even though my circumstances aren't what I hoped.

But I'm realizing that permission isn't coming from anyone else. I have to give it to myself.

Help me do that. Help me stop apologizing for being joyful. Help me stop feeling guilty for thriving in a season that doesn't match my expectations.

You've given me permission to live fully. Help me actually do it.

In Jesus' name, Amen.

TUESDAY PRAYER

Father, I've been treating this season like it's temporary.

Like it doesn't count. Like I'm not allowed to really invest in my life until circumstances change.

But that's a waste. This season is part of my story. And I'm allowed to make the most of it.

Give me courage to stop waiting and start building. To create a life I love right now instead of waiting for the "right time."

I don't need permission to thrive. I already have it.

In Jesus' name, Amen.

WEDNESDAY PRAYER

Lord, I've felt guilty for being happy while I'm single.

Like I'm not allowed to enjoy my life if it doesn't look the way I thought it would. Like thriving somehow means I've given up on my desires.

But that's not true. I can hope for more and still enjoy what I have. I can long for partnership and still build a meaningful life right now.

Help me release the guilt. Help me embrace the joy that's available to me today.

In Jesus' name, Amen.

THURSDAY PRAYER

God, what would it look like for me to thrive in this season?

Not just survive. Not just get by. But actually thrive.

Show me. What investments do I need to make? What dreams do I need to pursue? What parts of my life need attention that I've been ignoring?

I'm ready to build something meaningful. I'm ready to stop waiting and start living.

In Jesus' name, Amen.

FRIDAY PRAYER

Father, I'm giving myself permission.

Permission to be happy. Permission to thrive. Permission to build a life I love, even though my circumstances aren't what I hoped.

This isn't giving up on my desires. This is choosing to live fully in the season I'm actually in.

Give me courage to embrace this. To stop apologizing. To stop waiting.

I'm allowed to thrive. And I'm choosing to do it.

In Jesus' name, Amen.

SATURDAY PRAYER

God, I invested in my life this week.

I stopped treating this season like temporary housing and started building something meaningful. I gave myself permission to thrive, to be happy, to enjoy what I have.

And it felt good. It felt right. It felt like I was finally living instead of just waiting.

Help me keep going. Help me keep building. Help me keep thriving.

In Jesus' name, Amen.

SUNDAY REFLECTION

Reflect:

- Have you been waiting for permission to thrive? Where is that coming from?

- What would it look like to build a life you love right now, in this season?

Declare:

- I don't need permission to thrive.

- I'm allowed to be happy while I'm single.

- I'm building a meaningful life right now.

> **Carry This:** "You make known to me the path of life; you fill me with joy in your presence, with eternal pleasures at your right hand." , Psalm 16:11 (NIV)

SUNDAY PRAYER

God, I don't need permission to thrive.

You've already given it. And this week, I finally accepted it. I stopped apologizing for being happy. I stopped feeling guilty for enjoying my life.

I invested in this season. I built something meaningful. I allowed myself to thrive.

And I'm not going back to waiting. I'm living now. Fully. Joyfully. Without apology.

In Jesus' name, Amen.

WEEK 39: MAKING THE MOST OF THIS SEASON

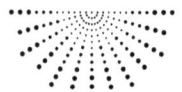

MONDAY DEVOTIONAL

This season won't last forever.

Whether it ends in a year or in ten years or never ends at all, it won't always look the way it does right now.

And one day, you're going to look back at this time and ask yourself a question: Did I make the most of it?

Did you steward it well? Did you invest in what mattered? Did you use the freedom, the time, the opportunities you had?

Or did you waste it wishing it was something else?

Ephesians 5:15-16 says,

> "Be very careful, then, how you live, not as unwise but as wise, making the most of every opportunity, because the days are evil" (NIV).

Making the most of every opportunity.

Not just the opportunities you wish you had. The ones you actually have.

You have opportunities right now that you won't have later. Time that's yours. Freedom to make decisions without consulting anyone else. Flexibility to pursue things that require undivided attention.

And if you spend this entire season resenting what you don't have, you're going to miss what you do have.

So what does it look like to make the most of this season?

It means you stop putting life on hold. You pursue dreams, build friendships, serve in ways that matter. You invest in your relationship with God. You develop skills, take risks, say yes to things that scare you.

It means you stop treating singleness like a problem to fix and start treating it like a season to steward.

Because it is.

This season has value. It has purpose. It has opportunities that are unique to right now.

And you're responsible for what you do with it.

One day, this season will end. And when it does, you'll either look back with gratitude for how you invested it, or with regret for how you wasted it.

The choice is yours.

Make the most of it.

MONDAY PRAYER

God, this season won't last forever.

And when it's over, I want to look back with gratitude, not regret. I want to know that I stewarded it well, that I invested in what mattered, that I made the most of the opportunities You gave me.

But I've been wasting it. Resenting it. Wishing it was something else.

Forgive me for that. Help me shift my perspective. Help me see this season as something valuable, something worth investing in, something I'll never have again.

I'm done wasting it. I'm ready to make the most of it.

In Jesus' name, Amen.

TUESDAY PRAYER

Father, what opportunities do I have right now that I won't have later?

What can I do in this season that I won't be able to do if my circumstances change? What should I be investing in, pursuing, building while I still have the freedom to do it?

Show me. Open my eyes to what's available right now. Help me steward these opportunities well.

In Jesus' name, Amen.

WEDNESDAY PRAYER

Lord, I've been putting life on hold.

Waiting for circumstances to change before I really start living. But that's a waste. This season matters. And I need to treat it like it does.

Give me courage to stop waiting and start investing. To pursue what matters. To build something meaningful right now.

I'm making the most of this season. Starting today.

In Jesus' name, Amen.

THURSDAY PRAYER

God, help me stop resenting this season.

I've been so focused on what I don't have that I've missed what I do have. I've been so busy wishing things were different that I haven't noticed the opportunities right in front of me.

Shift my perspective. Help me see this season as valuable. Help me steward it well instead of wasting it.

In Jesus' name, Amen.

FRIDAY PRAYER

Father, I'm investing in this season.

Not waiting for it to end. Not putting life on hold. Not treating it like something to survive.

I'm making the most of it. I'm pursuing what matters. I'm using the time, the freedom, the opportunities I have right now.

Help me stay intentional. Help me keep investing. Help me steward this season well.

In Jesus' name, Amen.

SATURDAY PRAYER

God, I made choices this week that mattered.

I stopped wasting time and started investing it. I pursued something meaningful. I used the opportunities I have instead of resenting the ones I don't.

And it felt good. It felt purposeful. It felt like I was finally stewarding this season well.

Help me keep going. Help me make the most of every day I have in this season.

In Jesus' name, Amen.

SUNDAY REFLECTION

Reflect:

- If this season ended tomorrow, would you look back with gratitude or regret?

- What's one way you can make the most of this season this week?

Declare:

- This season won't last forever, and I'm stewarding it well.

- I'm making the most of the opportunities I have right now.

- I will not waste this season wishing it was something else.

> **Carry This:** "Be very careful, then, how you live, not as unwise but as wise, making the most of every opportunity, because the days are evil.", Ephesians 5:15-16 (NIV)

SUNDAY PRAYER

God, I'm stewarding this season.

Not perfectly. Not without struggles. But intentionally. Purposefully. With gratitude for what I have instead of resentment for what I don't.

This week, I invested. I pursued. I made the most of opportunities I won't always have.

And when this season ends, I want to look back knowing I didn't waste it. Help me keep living that way.

In Jesus' name, Amen.

WEEK 40: CONTENTMENT AND ANTICIPATION TOGETHER

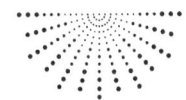

WEEK 40: Contentment and Anticipation Together

MONDAY DEVOTIONAL

You think contentment and anticipation are opposites.

That if you're content, you've given up hope. That if you're hoping for more, you can't be satisfied with what you have.

But that's not true.

You can be content in your current season and still hope for something different. You can be grateful for what you have and still desire more. You can find peace right now while still praying for change.

Contentment and anticipation aren't opposites. They're meant to coexist.

Philippians 4:11-13 shows this balance perfectly. Paul says,

> "I have learned to be content whatever the circumstances. I know what it is to be in need, and I know what it is to have plenty. I have learned the secret of being content in any and every situation,

> whether well fed or hungry, whether living in plenty or in want. I can do all this through him who gives me strength" (NIV).

Paul was content. But he was also working toward something. He was hoping for more, praying for more, actively pursuing his calling.

He didn't sit back and accept everything as it was. He kept moving, kept striving, kept believing God for more.

But in the middle of the pursuit, he found contentment.

That's the balance you need to find.

Contentment doesn't mean you stop praying for a relationship. It doesn't mean you pretend you don't want partnership. It doesn't mean you resign yourself to being single forever.

It means you stop tying your peace to whether or not your circumstances change.

You can hope for marriage and still find joy in singleness. You can pray for a partner and still build a meaningful life right now. You can anticipate change and still be grateful for what you have.

The key is learning to hold both at the same time.

When you only focus on contentment, you suppress desires God gave you. When you only focus on anticipation, you rob yourself of peace in the present.

But when you hold them together, you find freedom.

Freedom to hope without anxiety. Freedom to be grateful without giving up. Freedom to live fully right now while still believing God for more.

That's the balance worth fighting for.

MONDAY PRAYER

God, I've been treating contentment and hope like they're opposites.

I thought if I was content, I had to stop hoping. Or if I kept hoping, I couldn't be satisfied with what I have.

But that's not true. And that false choice has been making me miserable.

Teach me to hold both. Teach me to be content in this season while still praying for change. Teach me to find peace right now while still hoping for more.

I don't want to suppress my desires. But I also don't want to lose my peace waiting for them to be fulfilled.

Help me find the balance.

In Jesus' name, Amen.

TUESDAY PRAYER

Father, I've been tying my peace to my circumstances.

When things look hopeful, I'm happy. When nothing changes, I'm miserable. My emotions ride the rollercoaster of my situation.

But that's not contentment. That's instability.

Teach me to anchor my peace in You, not in whether my circumstances match my desires. Teach me to be content because You're good, not because my life is going well.

I want peace that holds, no matter what happens.

In Jesus' name, Amen.

WEDNESDAY PRAYER

Lord, I'm afraid that if I'm content, I'll stop hoping.

That if I find peace in singleness, I'll somehow signal to You that I don't want marriage anymore. That contentment means giving up.

But that's not what contentment is. Contentment is trusting You while I wait. It's finding peace in Your presence even when my desires aren't fulfilled yet.

Help me be content without giving up hope. Help me rest without resigning.

In Jesus' name, Amen.

THURSDAY PRAYER

God, help me stop making my desires the enemy.

I've been so afraid of wanting too much that I've tried to kill the desire altogether. I've told myself that if I stop wanting marriage, I'll finally find peace.

But that's not contentment. That's suppression.

You gave me the desire for partnership. It's not wrong. It's not something I need to kill.

Teach me to hold my desires with open hands. To want what I want without demanding it. To hope without insisting on my timeline.

In Jesus' name, Amen.

FRIDAY PRAYER

Father, I'm learning to hold both.

Contentment and anticipation. Gratitude and hope. Peace in the present and faith for the future.

It's hard. I want to collapse into one or the other. But You're teaching me that I can have both.

Help me stay in this tension. Help me be grateful for what I have while still praying for what I don't have yet.

I'm content. And I'm hopeful. At the same time.

In Jesus' name, Amen.

SATURDAY PRAYER

God, I found the balance this week.

I stopped treating contentment and hope like they're opposites. I let myself hope for more while still finding peace in what I have.

And it changed things. I felt lighter. Less desperate. More at peace.

Help me stay here. When I'm tempted to collapse into one extreme or the other, bring me back to this balance.

Contentment and anticipation. Together.

In Jesus' name, Amen.

SUNDAY REFLECTION

Reflect:

- Have you been treating contentment and hope like opposites? How has that affected you?

- What would it look like to be content in your current season while still hoping for more?

Declare:

- Contentment and anticipation can coexist.

- I can be grateful for what I have while still praying for more.

- My peace doesn't depend on my circumstances changing.

Carry This: "I have learned to be content whatever the circumstances.", Philippians 4:11b (NIV)

SUNDAY PRAYER

God, You're teaching me a new kind of peace.

Peace that doesn't depend on my circumstances. Peace that holds even when my desires aren't fulfilled yet. Peace that coexists with hope instead of replacing it.

This week, I learned to be content and hopeful at the same time. And it felt like freedom.

Help me keep living this way. Help me hold both without collapsing into either extreme.

In Jesus' name, Amen.

WEEK 41: SURRENDERING YOUR TIMELINE TO GOD

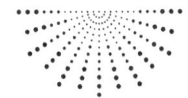

MONDAY DEVOTIONAL

You've been holding onto your timeline with white knuckles.

You had a plan. You thought you'd be married by a certain age. You thought things would happen in a certain order. You thought God was working on your schedule.

And when He didn't, you got angry. Frustrated. Desperate.

Because you've been trying to control what was never yours to control.

Your timeline isn't yours. It's God's. And until you surrender it, you're going to stay stuck in frustration, anxiety, and disappointment.

> Proverbs 16:9 says, "In their hearts humans plan their course, but the Lord establishes their steps" (NIV).

You plan. God establishes.

You set the timeline. God determines the timing.

And the sooner you surrender control, the sooner you'll find peace.

Surrendering your timeline doesn't mean you stop hoping for marriage. It doesn't mean you give up on your desires. It doesn't mean you pretend you don't care when things happen.

It means you release the demand that God work on your schedule.

It means you stop insisting that marriage happens by a certain age, that your life follows a certain order, that God meets your deadlines.

It means you trust that His timing is better than yours, even when you can't see it.

This is hard. Because control feels safer than trust. Having a plan feels more secure than surrendering to someone else's.

But your plan doesn't account for what God knows. Your timeline doesn't consider what He's preparing you for. Your schedule doesn't factor in His purposes.

And when you cling to your timeline, you miss what He's doing in His.

So what does surrender look like?

It looks like praying, "God, I want this. But I trust Your timing more than mine."

It looks like releasing the age, the deadline, the specific order you thought things would happen.

It looks like choosing peace over control, trust over certainty, faith over fear.

Your timeline is in God's hands. And that's exactly where it should be.

MONDAY PRAYER

God, I've been holding onto my timeline too tightly.

I've had a plan, an age, a deadline. And when You didn't follow it, I got angry. I felt betrayed. I questioned whether You were good.

But my timeline was never Yours. And clinging to it has kept me stuck in frustration.

I'm releasing it. All of it. The age I thought I'd be married by. The order I thought things would happen. The deadline I've been imposing on You.

I trust Your timing more than mine. Even when I don't understand it.

In Jesus' name, Amen.

TUESDAY PRAYER

Father, I don't understand Your timing.

I've been ready for years. I've been praying, waiting, hoping. And nothing's changed.

And I'm honest enough to admit that it makes me doubt. Doubt Your goodness. Doubt whether You're listening. Doubt whether You care.

But my confusion doesn't change who You are. You're still good. You're still working. You're still in control.

Help me trust You when I don't understand. Help me surrender my timeline even when it doesn't make sense.

In Jesus' name, Amen.

WEDNESDAY PRAYER

Lord, control feels safer than trust.

If I have a plan, I feel secure. If I can control the timing, I feel less anxious.

But that's not faith. That's fear.

Teach me to trust You with my timeline. Teach me that Your timing is better than mine, even when it's slower. Teach me that surrendering control is actually safer than clinging to it.

You know what I don't know. And I'm choosing to trust that.

In Jesus' name, Amen.

THURSDAY PRAYER

God, help me stop comparing my timeline to everyone else's.

They got married at 23. I'm still single at 30. They met someone right away. I've been waiting for years.

And comparing timelines is destroying me.

Remind me that my story is mine. That Your timing for me is different than Your timing for them. That comparison steals my peace and my ability to trust You.

My timeline is Yours. And theirs has nothing to do with mine.

In Jesus' name, Amen.

FRIDAY PRAYER

Father, I'm surrendering my timeline.

Not because I don't care when things happen. Not because I'm giving up hope. But because I trust You more than I trust my plan.

I release the age. I release the deadline. I release the order I thought things would happen.

Your timing is better than mine. And I'm choosing to believe that, even when it's hard.

In Jesus' name, Amen.

SATURDAY PRAYER

God, I let go this week.

I stopped demanding that You work on my schedule. I stopped insisting on my timeline. I released control.

And even though it's scary, it's also freeing. Because I'm not carrying the weight of making things happen anymore.

Help me stay surrendered. When I'm tempted to take control back, remind me that Your timing is better.

In Jesus' name, Amen.

SUNDAY REFLECTION

Reflect:

- What timeline have you been imposing on God? What age, deadline, or order are you clinging to?

- What would it look like to fully surrender your timeline to Him?

Declare:

- My timeline is in God's hands, not mine.

- I trust His timing more than my plan.

- Surrendering control is safer than clinging to it.

> **Carry This:** "In their hearts humans plan their course, but the Lord establishes their steps.", Proverbs 16:9 (NIV)

SUNDAY PRAYER

God, my timeline is in Your hands.

I've released it. I've stopped demanding that You work on my schedule. I've surrendered control.

And I'm finding peace in that surrender. Not because I know when things will happen, but because I know who's in control.

Your timing is better than mine. And I'm trusting You with it.

In Jesus' name, Amen.

WEEK 42: TRUSTING HIS TIMING WHEN IT DOESN'T MAKE SENSE

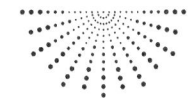

MONDAY DEVOTIONAL

God's timing rarely makes sense.

You've been ready for years. You've done the work, healed the wounds, become the person you think you need to be. And still, nothing's changed.

Meanwhile, people who seem less prepared, less mature, less ready are getting exactly what you've been praying for.

And it doesn't make sense.

You want to trust God's timing. You want to believe He knows what He's doing. But when you look at your life, when you watch everyone else move forward while you stay stuck, trust feels impossible.

Isaiah 55:8-9 says,

> "'For my thoughts are not your thoughts, neither are your ways my ways,' declares the Lord. 'As the heavens are higher than the earth, so are my ways higher than your ways and my thoughts than your thoughts'" (NIV).

His ways are higher. His thoughts are different. His timing operates on a level you can't fully understand.

And that's frustrating. Because you want it to make sense. You want to see the logic, understand the delay, know why He's waiting.

But faith doesn't require understanding. It requires trust.

Trusting God's timing when it doesn't make sense means you believe He's good even when His plan looks nothing like yours. It means you hold onto His character when His choices confuse you. It means you anchor yourself in who He is, not in what He's doing.

Because what He's doing might not make sense for years. Maybe not until you're on the other side looking back. Maybe not until eternity.

But who He is never changes. He's good. He's faithful. He's working for your good, even when you can't see it.

So how do you trust when it doesn't make sense?

You stop demanding explanations. You stop insisting that God justify His timing. You stop making your understanding a requirement for your faith.

And you choose to trust Him anyway.

Not because you understand. But because you know Him.

MONDAY PRAYER

God, Your timing doesn't make sense.

I've been ready for years. I've done everything I know to do. And still, nothing's changed.

Meanwhile, people who seem less prepared are getting what I've been praying for. And I don't understand it.

Help me trust You anyway. Help me believe You're good even when Your plan confuses me. Help me anchor myself in who You are instead of demanding to understand what You're doing.

Your ways are higher than mine. And I'm choosing to trust that, even when I don't understand.

In Jesus' name, Amen.

TUESDAY PRAYER

Father, I want explanations.

I want to know why You're waiting. I want to understand the delay. I want the logic to make sense.

But You're not giving me that. And trying to force understanding is just making me more frustrated.

Teach me to trust without needing to understand. Teach me that faith doesn't require explanations. Teach me that Your character is enough, even when Your choices confuse me.

I don't understand Your timing. But I'm choosing to trust You anyway.

In Jesus' name, Amen.

WEDNESDAY PRAYER

Lord, I watch other people get what I'm praying for.

And it makes me question everything. Are they more deserving? Did they do something I didn't? Did I miss something?

But that's not how You work. You're not ranking us, comparing us, rewarding based on performance.

Your timing for them is different than Your timing for me. And comparing our stories is destroying my ability to trust You.

Help me stop looking at their timeline and focus on Yours for me. Help me trust that You're working in my story, even when it looks different than theirs.

In Jesus' name, Amen.

THURSDAY PRAYER

God, help me hold onto Your character when Your choices confuse me.

I know You're good. I know You're faithful. I know You love me.

But when Your timing doesn't make sense, I start to doubt all of that.

Anchor me in who You are. Remind me of what You've already done. Remind me that Your goodness doesn't depend on whether I understand Your plan.

You're good. Even when Your timing confuses me.

In Jesus' name, Amen.

FRIDAY PRAYER

Father, I'm choosing trust over understanding.

I don't understand Your timing. I don't see the purpose in the delay. I don't know why You're waiting.

But I know You. And that's enough.

Help me release the need for explanations. Help me stop demanding that Your timing make sense to me. Help me trust You based on who You are, not based on whether I can understand what You're doing.

Your ways are higher than mine. And I'm trusting that.

In Jesus' name, Amen.

SATURDAY PRAYER

God, I stopped demanding explanations this week.

I stopped insisting that Your timing make sense. I stopped trying to force understanding.

And I found a different kind of peace. Not the peace of knowing why, but the peace of knowing who.

You're good. You're faithful. You're working for my good. And that's enough, even when I don't understand.

In Jesus' name, Amen.

SUNDAY REFLECTION

Reflect:

- Where has God's timing confused you? What doesn't make sense?

- What would it look like to trust Him based on His character instead of your understanding?

Declare:

- God's timing doesn't have to make sense for me to trust Him.

- His ways are higher than mine.

- I trust His character, even when His choices confuse me.

> **Carry This:** "'For my thoughts are not your thoughts, neither are your ways my ways,' declares the Lord.", Isaiah 55:8 (NIV)

SUNDAY PRAYER

God, Your timing doesn't have to make sense for me to trust You.

This week, I learned that faith doesn't require understanding. That I can trust You based on Your character, not based on whether I can explain Your choices.

I don't understand why You're waiting. But I know You're good. And I'm anchoring myself in that.

Your ways are higher than mine. And I'm choosing to trust You anyway.

In Jesus' name, Amen.

WEEK 43: PREPARING FOR WHATEVER COMES NEXT

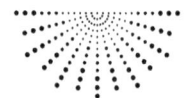

MONDAY DEVOTIONAL

You don't know what's coming next.

You might get married next year. You might stay single for another decade. You might be called to lifelong singleness. You might meet someone tomorrow.

You don't know.

And that uncertainty has been paralyzing you. Because you want to prepare for the right thing, and you're afraid of wasting time preparing for the wrong thing.

But here's what you're missing: preparation isn't wasted, no matter what comes next.

Every area you grow in, every wound you heal, every skill you develop, every character quality you strengthen will serve you in whatever season comes next.

Married or single, you'll need emotional health. You'll need strong character. You'll need spiritual maturity. You'll need the ability to love well, set boundaries, and handle conflict.

So stop waiting to find out what's coming before you start preparing. Prepare now for whatever God has next.

2 Timothy 2:21 says,

> **"Those who cleanse themselves from the latter will be instruments for special purposes, made holy, useful to the Master and prepared to do any good work" (NIV).**

Prepared to do any good work.

Not prepared for one specific outcome. Prepared for whatever God calls you to.

What does that look like practically?

It means you work on yourself. You deal with wounds instead of ignoring them. You develop character instead of coasting. You grow spiritually instead of stagnating.

It means you don't put life on hold waiting to find out what's next. You invest in yourself now, trusting that whatever comes, you'll be ready for it.

It means you prepare for marriage by becoming someone who can love well. And you prepare for continued singleness by building a life worth living.

Either way, the preparation matters.

You don't know what's coming. But you can be ready for it anyway.

MONDAY PRAYER

God, I don't know what's coming next.

And that uncertainty has been paralyzing me. I've been afraid to prepare for the wrong thing, so I haven't been preparing for anything.

But I'm realizing that preparation isn't wasted. That growing, healing, and developing character will serve me no matter what comes next.

Help me stop waiting to find out what's coming before I start preparing. Help me invest in myself now, trusting that whatever You have next, I'll be ready for it.

In Jesus' name, Amen.

TUESDAY PRAYER

Father, show me what I need to work on.

What wounds need healing? What character needs developing? What areas need growth?

I don't want to waste this time. I want to prepare well for whatever comes next.

Give me clarity about where to invest my energy. Show me what matters most.

In Jesus' name, Amen.

WEDNESDAY PRAYER

Lord, I've been putting work on hold.

Waiting to see if I need to prepare for marriage or for continued singleness. Waiting to find out what's coming before I commit to growth.

But that's a waste. Whatever comes, I'll need to be whole. I'll need to be healthy. I'll need to be mature.

Help me do the work now instead of waiting. Help me prepare for whatever comes next by becoming who You're calling me to be.

In Jesus' name, Amen.

THURSDAY PRAYER

God, help me focus on what I can control.

I can't control what's coming next. I can't control the timeline. I can't control whether I get married or stay single.

But I can control how I prepare. I can control whether I grow. I can control whether I deal with my issues or ignore them.

Give me the discipline to focus on what I can actually control. To prepare well for whatever You have next.

In Jesus' name, Amen.

FRIDAY PRAYER

Father, I'm preparing now.

Not because I know what's coming. But because I don't. And whatever comes, I want to be ready.

I'm working on myself. I'm healing wounds. I'm developing character. I'm growing spiritually.

And I'm trusting that this preparation isn't wasted, no matter what happens next.

In Jesus' name, Amen.

SATURDAY PRAYER

God, I invested in myself this week.

I stopped waiting to find out what's coming and started preparing for whatever it is. I worked on areas that need growth. I dealt with wounds I've been ignoring.

And it felt productive. Like I was finally moving forward instead of staying stuck.

Help me keep preparing. Help me keep growing. Help me be ready for whatever comes next.

In Jesus' name, Amen.

SUNDAY REFLECTION

Reflect:

- What areas do you need to work on that will serve you no matter what comes next?

- What have you been putting on hold waiting to find out what's coming?

Declare:

- Preparation isn't wasted, no matter what comes next.

- I'm becoming ready for whatever God has for me.

- I will invest in myself now instead of waiting.

> **Carry This: "Those who cleanse themselves from the latter will be instruments for special purposes, made holy, useful to the Master and prepared to do any good work.", 2 Timothy 2:21 (NIV)**

SUNDAY PRAYER

God, I'm ready for whatever comes next.

Not because I know what it is. But because I've been preparing. Growing. Healing. Developing.

This week, I stopped putting work on hold and started investing in who I'm becoming. And I'm trusting that whatever You have next, I'll be ready for it.

In Jesus' name, Amen.

WEEK 44: PRAYING FOR YOUR FUTURE (MARRIAGE OR SINGLENESS)

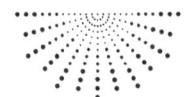

MONDAY DEVOTIONAL

You're allowed to pray for what you want.

God isn't offended by your desire for marriage. He's not disappointed that you're hoping for partnership. He doesn't need you to pretend you're content with singleness if that's not the calling He's given you.

But you also need to hold your prayers with open hands.

Because what you want might not be what's best. And God loves you too much to give you something just because you asked for it.

Matthew 7:7-8 says,

> "Ask and it will be given to you; seek and you will find; knock and the door will be opened to you. For everyone who asks receives; the one who seeks finds; and to the one who knocks, the door will be opened" (NIV).

Ask. Seek. Knock.

God invites you to bring your desires to Him. To pray honestly about what you want. To ask for what you're hoping for.

But He never promises to give you exactly what you ask for in exactly the way you want it.

Because He's not a vending machine. He's a Father. And sometimes the most loving thing a Father can do is say no.

So how do you pray for your future when you don't know what it holds?

You pray for wisdom. You pray for clarity. You pray that God will guide you toward His will, whether that's marriage or singleness.

You pray for a godly spouse if that's His plan for you. You describe what you're hoping for, what matters to you, what kind of partnership you're seeking.

But you also pray for contentment in whatever He gives. You pray for the grace to thrive whether you're married or single. You pray that His will becomes more important to you than your own.

And you trust that whatever He chooses is better than what you would have chosen for yourself.

Because it is.

MONDAY PRAYER

God, I'm bringing You my desires.

I want marriage. I want partnership. I want someone to share my life with.

And I'm not going to pretend I don't. I'm not going to hide what I'm hoping for or act like I'm content when I'm not.

But I'm also holding this with open hands. I'm asking You to give me what's best, not just what I want. I'm trusting that if marriage is Your plan for me, You'll bring it in the right timing. And if singleness is Your calling for me, You'll give me the grace to thrive in it.

Your will, not mine. But I'm still asking.

In Jesus' name, Amen.

TUESDAY PRAYER

Father, if marriage is Your plan for me, I'm praying for my future spouse.

Wherever they are, whatever they're walking through, meet them there. Grow them. Heal them. Prepare them for what's coming.

And prepare me too. Make me into someone who can love well, who can build a healthy partnership, who can walk in covenant faithfully.

I don't know if marriage is Your plan. But if it is, I'm asking You to be working in both of us, making us ready.

In Jesus' name, Amen.

WEDNESDAY PRAYER

Lord, if singleness is Your calling for me, give me grace to embrace it.

Not just to tolerate it. Not just to survive it. But to thrive in it.

Show me the unique purpose You have for me in this calling. Show me the freedom, the opportunities, the impact I can have that I wouldn't have if my life looked different.

And give me peace. Deep, lasting peace that doesn't depend on my circumstances changing.

If this is Your plan for me, help me walk in it joyfully.

In Jesus' name, Amen.

THURSDAY PRAYER

God, I don't know which path is Yours for me.

I don't know if I'm praying for marriage when You've called me to singleness. Or if I'm praying for contentment in singleness when marriage is just around the corner.

So I'm asking for wisdom. For clarity. For You to guide me toward Your will, whatever it is.

And I'm trusting that You'll make it clear in Your timing.

In Jesus' name, Amen.

FRIDAY PRAYER

Father, Your will matters more than mine.

I have desires. I have hopes. I have prayers I've been praying for years.

But more than getting what I want, I want what You want for me. Because Your plan is better than mine. Your timing is better than mine. Your will is perfect, even when I don't understand it.

So I'm surrendering my desires to You. Do what's best. Even if it's not what I'm asking for.

In Jesus' name, Amen.

SATURDAY PRAYER

God, I prayed honestly this week.

I brought You my desires without pretending. I asked for what I want. But I also surrendered to Your will.

And there's freedom in that. Freedom to hope without demanding. Freedom to ask without insisting. Freedom to desire without controlling.

Help me keep praying this way. Honest about what I want. Surrendered to what You choose.

In Jesus' name, Amen.

SUNDAY REFLECTION

Reflect:

- Have you been praying honestly about what you want? Or have you been suppressing your desires?

- What would it look like to hold your prayers with open hands, trusting God's will over your own?

Declare:

- I'm allowed to pray for what I want.

- I trust God's will more than my own desires.

- Whatever He chooses for me is better than what I would choose for myself.

> **Carry This:** "Ask and it will be given to you; seek and you will find; knock and the door will be opened to you.", Matthew 7:7 (NIV)

SUNDAY PRAYER

God, I'm trusting You with my future.

I've prayed for what I want. I've asked for marriage if that's Your plan. I've asked for grace if singleness is Your calling.

And now I'm releasing it. I'm trusting that whatever You choose is better than what I would choose for myself.

Your will, not mine. And I'm at peace with that.

In Jesus' name, Amen.

WEEK 46: WHEN WAITING FEELS ENDLESS

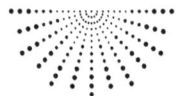

MONDAY DEVOTIONAL

You're tired of waiting.

You've been faithful. You've been patient. You've done everything you know to do. And still, nothing's changed.

And you're starting to wonder if it ever will.

Waiting is hard. Especially when you don't know what you're waiting for or how long it will last. Especially when everyone around you is getting what you're praying for. Especially when the waiting feels endless.

But here's what you need to remember: waiting isn't wasted time.

God is working in the waiting. He's shaping you, preparing you, building something in you that you'll need for whatever comes next.

Isaiah 40:31 says,

> "But those who hope in the Lord will renew their strength. They will soar on wings like eagles; they will run and not grow weary, they will walk and not be faint" (NIV).

Those who hope in the Lord.

Not those who hope in their circumstances changing. Not those who hope in their timeline being fulfilled.

Those who hope in the Lord.

Because circumstances might not change. Your timeline might not be met. But God is constant. And anchoring your hope in Him means you can endure the waiting without losing yourself in it.

So how do you keep going when waiting feels endless?

You stop measuring progress by whether your circumstances have changed. You start measuring it by who you're becoming in the process.

You stop asking, "When will this end?" and start asking, "What is God doing in me right now?"

You stop tying your hope to outcomes and start tying it to God's character.

Waiting is hard. But it's not wasted. And it won't last forever.

Even when it feels like it will.

MONDAY PRAYER

God, I'm tired of waiting.

I've been patient. I've been faithful. I've done everything I know to do. And still, nothing's changed.

And I'm starting to lose hope.

Remind me that waiting isn't wasted. Remind me that You're working in this season, even when I can't see it. Remind me that my hope is in You, not in my circumstances changing.

Give me strength to keep going. Give me endurance when I want to give up. Give me hope that holds, even when waiting feels endless.

In Jesus' name, Amen.

TUESDAY PRAYER

Father, I don't know how much longer I can do this.

The waiting feels unbearable. The uncertainty is exhausting. The watching everyone else move forward while I stay stuck is crushing me.

But I know You're not asking me to wait forever. Just today. Just this moment. Just one more step.

Help me take it. Give me strength for today, not for the entire journey. Help me keep going, one day at a time.

In Jesus' name, Amen.

WEDNESDAY PRAYER

Lord, what are You doing in the waiting?

I've been so focused on when it will end that I haven't stopped to ask what You're doing in it.

What are You teaching me? What are You building in me? What am I learning in this season that I couldn't learn any other way?

Open my eyes to see what You're doing. Help me stop wasting the waiting by only resenting it.

In Jesus' name, Amen.

THURSDAY PRAYER

God, help me measure progress differently.

I've been measuring progress by whether my circumstances have changed. And by that measure, I haven't made any.

But maybe progress isn't about circumstances. Maybe it's about character. About who I'm becoming. About how I'm handling the waiting.

Help me see the progress I'm actually making. Help me celebrate growth that has nothing to do with whether I'm still single.

In Jesus' name, Amen.

FRIDAY PRAYER

Father, I'm anchoring my hope in You.

Not in my circumstances changing. Not in my timeline being met. But in You.

You're constant. You're faithful. You're working for my good, even when I can't see it.

And that's where my hope needs to be. Not in outcomes, but in You.

Help me hold onto that when waiting feels endless.

In Jesus' name, Amen.

SATURDAY PRAYER

God, I made it through another week.

The waiting still feels hard. The uncertainty still weighs on me. But I'm still here. Still trusting. Still hoping.

And that's something.

Give me strength for the next week. For the next day. For the next moment.

I'm not giving up. I'm still waiting. And I'm trusting You with the timing.

In Jesus' name, Amen.

SUNDAY REFLECTION

Reflect:

- How are you measuring progress? By circumstances or by character?

- What might God be doing in the waiting that you've been missing?

Declare:

- Waiting isn't wasted time.

- My hope is in God, not in my circumstances changing.

- I will endure the waiting without losing myself in it.

Carry This:

> "But those who hope in the Lord will renew their strength. They will soar on wings like eagles; they will run and not grow weary, they will walk and not be faint.", Isaiah 40:31 (NIV)

SUNDAY PRAYER

God, waiting feels endless.

But You've carried me through another week. You've given me strength I didn't think I had. You've sustained hope when I thought it was gone.

I don't know how much longer this will last. But I know You're with me in it. And that has to be enough.

Help me keep going. Keep hoping. Keep trusting. One day at a time.

In Jesus' name, Amen.

WEEK 47: HOPE THAT DOESN'T DISAPPOINT

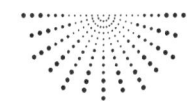

MONDAY DEVOTIONAL

You've been disappointed so many times that you're afraid to hope again.

Every time you let yourself believe something might change, it didn't. Every time you got your hopes up, they got crushed. Every time you thought, "Maybe this is it," it wasn't.

So you've stopped hoping. Because disappointment hurts too much.

But the problem isn't hope. The problem is what you've been hoping in.

You've been hoping in outcomes. In circumstances. In people. In timelines. And all of those will disappoint you eventually.

But there's a hope that doesn't disappoint. And it's not based on anything changing.

Romans 5:3-5 says,

> "Not only so, but we also glory in our sufferings, because we know that suffering produces perseverance; perseverance, character; and

character, hope. And hope does not put us to shame, because God's love has been poured out into our hearts through the Holy Spirit, who has been given to us" (NIV).

Hope does not put us to shame.

This kind of hope isn't based on getting what you want. It's based on who God is.

It's hope that He's good, even when life isn't. Hope that He's working, even when you can't see it. Hope that He loves you, even when your circumstances don't reflect it.

That kind of hope doesn't disappoint. Because it's not dependent on anything changing. It's dependent on God remaining who He's always been.

So how do you hope again after so much disappointment?

You shift what you're hoping in. You stop tying hope to outcomes and start tying it to God's character.

You stop saying, "I hope I get married soon," and start saying, "I hope in God's goodness, whether I get married or not."

You stop hoping for circumstances to change and start hoping in the One who holds your circumstances.

That's the hope that doesn't disappoint. Because God never fails.

MONDAY PRAYER

God, I'm afraid to hope again.

I've been disappointed too many times. I've let myself believe things would change, and they didn't. I've gotten my hopes up, and they've been crushed.

So I've stopped hoping. Because it hurts too much.

But I know that's not the answer. Teach me to hope differently. Teach me to hope in You instead of in outcomes. Teach me that hope anchored in Your character never disappoints.

I want to hope again. But I need You to show me how.

In Jesus' name, Amen.

TUESDAY PRAYER

Father, I've been hoping in the wrong things.

I've been hoping in circumstances changing. In timelines being met. In outcomes going my way.

And all of those have disappointed me.

Teach me to hope in You instead. In Your goodness. In Your faithfulness. In Your love that doesn't change based on my circumstances.

That's the hope that won't disappoint me. And that's where I need to anchor.

In Jesus' name, Amen.

WEDNESDAY PRAYER

Lord, help me separate hope from expectation.

I've been confusing the two. I've expected outcomes, and when they didn't happen, I felt like hope failed me.

But hope isn't about demanding outcomes. It's about trusting You with them.

Teach me to hope in You without demanding specific results. Teach me that hope can coexist with uncertainty.

In Jesus' name, Amen.

THURSDAY PRAYER

God, I want to hope again.

Not naively. Not by pretending disappointment doesn't hurt. But by anchoring hope in something that won't fail.

You won't fail. Your character won't change. Your love won't run out.

And that's what I'm choosing to hope in. Not in circumstances. In You.

Help me rebuild hope on a foundation that holds.

In Jesus' name, Amen.

FRIDAY PRAYER

Father, Your love has been poured into my heart.

And that love is the foundation of hope that doesn't disappoint. Not because circumstances always go my way. But because You're always good.

Remind me of that when disappointment comes. Remind me that my hope is in You, not in outcomes.

You're faithful. And that's the hope I'm holding onto.

In Jesus' name, Amen.

SATURDAY PRAYER

God, I'm learning to hope differently.

This week, I stopped hoping in outcomes and started hoping in You. I stopped tying hope to circumstances and started anchoring it in Your character.

And it feels different. Safer. More solid.

Help me keep hoping this way. When disappointment comes again, remind me where my hope actually belongs.

In Jesus' name, Amen.

SUNDAY REFLECTION

Reflect:

- What have you been hoping in that keeps disappointing you?

- What would it look like to hope in God's character instead of in outcomes?

Declare:

- Hope anchored in God's character doesn't disappoint.

- I will hope in who God is, not in what He gives.

- God's faithfulness is the foundation of my hope.

> **Carry This:** "And hope does not put us to shame, because God's love has been poured out into our hearts through the Holy Spirit, who has been given to us.", Romans 5:5 (NIV)

SUNDAY PRAYER

God, hope anchored in You doesn't disappoint.

This week, I learned that. I shifted what I was hoping in, and I found a hope that holds.

I don't know if my circumstances will change. But I know You won't. And that's enough.

Help me keep hoping. Not naively. But deeply. In You.

In Jesus' name, Amen.

WEEK 48: BELIEVING GOD'S PROMISES OVER YOUR FEELINGS

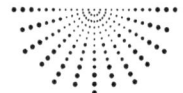

MONDAY DEVOTIONAL

Your feelings are lying to you.

They're telling you God has forgotten you. That you're running out of time. That nothing's ever going to change. That you're destined to be alone forever.

And some days, those feelings are so loud that they drown out everything else.

But feelings aren't facts. And God's promises are more reliable than your emotions.

Numbers 23:19 says,

> "God is not human, that he should lie, not a human being, that he should change his mind. Does he speak and then not act? Does he promise and not fulfill?" (NIV).

Does he promise and not fulfill?

The answer is no. God keeps His promises. Every single one.

But here's where it gets tricky: God's promises aren't always what you think they are.

He didn't promise you'd be married by a certain age. He didn't promise your life would follow a specific timeline. He didn't promise you'd get exactly what you're praying for in exactly the way you want it.

But He did promise He'd never leave you. He promised to work all things for your good. He promised His plans for you are good. He promised His love never fails.

Those are the promises you need to anchor yourself in. Not the ones you made up. The ones He actually gave.

And when your feelings contradict God's promises, you have to choose which one you're going to believe.

Your feelings will tell you God isn't good because your life doesn't look the way you want. God's promise says He's good regardless of your circumstances.

Your feelings will tell you you're forgotten. God's promise says He knows every hair on your head.

Your feelings will tell you nothing will ever change. God's promise says He's making all things new.

Which voice are you listening to?

Because the voice you listen to will determine how you live. If you believe your feelings, you'll live in despair, anxiety, and hopelessness. If you believe God's promises, you'll live in faith, peace, and hope.

Your feelings are real. But they're not reliable.

God's promises are both.

MONDAY PRAYER

God, my feelings are louder than Your promises.

They tell me I'm forgotten. They tell me nothing will ever change. They tell me I'm running out of time.

And some days, I believe them more than I believe You.

Forgive me for that. Forgive me for trusting my emotions more than Your Word. Forgive me for letting feelings dictate my faith.

Teach me to anchor myself in Your promises instead of in my feelings. Teach me to believe what You say over what I feel.

Your promises are true. Help me live like I believe that.

In Jesus' name, Amen.

TUESDAY PRAYER

Father, what are Your actual promises?

Not the ones I've made up. Not the ones I've assumed. The ones You've actually given.

You promised to never leave me. You promised to work all things for my good. You promised Your plans for me are good.

Help me anchor myself in those promises instead of creating my own and then being disappointed when they're not fulfilled.

Your promises are enough. Help me believe that.

In Jesus' name, Amen.

WEDNESDAY PRAYER

Lord, my feelings say You've forgotten me.

But Your promise says You know every hair on my head. That You see the sparrow fall. That I matter to You.

My feelings lie. But Your Word is truth.

Help me believe Your Word over my feelings. Help me trust Your promises when my emotions contradict them.

You haven't forgotten me. And I'm choosing to believe that, even when I don't feel it.

In Jesus' name, Amen.

THURSDAY PRAYER

God, help me stop waiting to feel before I believe.

I've been waiting for my emotions to line up with Your promises before I'll trust them. I've been demanding to feel Your presence before I'll believe You're with me.

But faith doesn't work that way. Faith believes before it feels. Faith trusts what You say, whether emotions confirm it or not.

Teach me to believe Your promises even when I don't feel them. Teach me that feelings follow faith, not the other way around.

In Jesus' name, Amen.

FRIDAY PRAYER

Father, I'm choosing Your promises over my feelings.

My feelings say I'm alone. Your promise says You're with me.

My feelings say nothing will change. Your promise says You're making all things new.

My feelings say I'm forgotten. Your promise says I'm engraved on the palms of Your hands.

I'm believing Your Word. Not my emotions.

In Jesus' name, Amen.

SATURDAY PRAYER

God, I anchored myself in Your promises this week.

And it changed how I processed my emotions. Instead of letting feelings dictate my reality, I filtered them through Your truth.

My feelings still fluctuate. But my foundation doesn't. Because it's built on Your Word, not on my emotions.

Help me keep choosing this. When feelings try to override truth, bring me back to Your promises.

In Jesus' name, Amen.

SUNDAY REFLECTION

Reflect:

- What are your feelings telling you that contradicts God's promises?

- Which of God's actual promises do you need to anchor yourself in?

Declare:

- My feelings are real, but they're not always reliable.

- God's promises are both real and reliable.

- I will believe God's Word over my emotions.

> **Carry This:** "God is not human, that he should lie, not a human being, that he should change his mind. Does he speak and then not act? Does he promise and not fulfill?", Numbers 23:19 (NIV)

SUNDAY PRAYER

God, Your promises are more reliable than my feelings.

This week, I learned to filter my emotions through Your Word instead of letting emotions determine what I believe.

My feelings will lie. But Your promises never do.

Help me keep anchoring myself in truth. Help me believe what You say, even when I don't feel it.

Your Word is my foundation. And it holds.

In Jesus' name, Amen.

WEEK 51: LOOKING AHEAD WITH FAITH

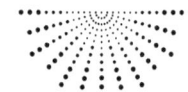

MONDAY DEVOTIONAL

You don't know what next year holds.

You don't know if you'll still be single. You don't know if circumstances will change. You don't know what God is preparing you for.

But you can look ahead with faith anyway.

Not blind optimism. Not naive hope that ignores reality. But faith that trusts God with the unknown.

Hebrews 11:1 says,

> "Now faith is confidence in what we hope for and assurance about what we do not see" (NIV).

Assurance about what we do not see.

You can't see the future. But you can trust the One who holds it.

Looking ahead with faith doesn't mean you know what's coming. It means you know who's in control. It means you trust that God is good, that He's working for your benefit, that His plans are better than yours.

It means you walk into the unknown with confidence, not because the path is clear, but because the Guide is faithful.

So what does that look like practically?

It means you stop demanding to know the future before you'll trust God with it. It means you release control and embrace uncertainty. It means you choose faith over fear.

It means you say, "I don't know what's coming. But I know who's with me. And that's enough."

Looking ahead with faith doesn't eliminate uncertainty. It just changes how you carry it.

You walk into the unknown with peace instead of panic. With hope instead of dread. With trust instead of control.

Because the future is uncertain. But God isn't.

And that makes all the difference.

MONDAY PRAYER

God, I don't know what next year holds.

I don't know if I'll still be single. I don't know if circumstances will change. I don't know what You're preparing me for.

But I'm choosing to look ahead with faith anyway. Not because I can see the future, but because I trust You with it.

You're in control. You're working for my good. Your plans are better than mine.

And that's enough. Even when I don't know what's coming.

In Jesus' name, Amen.

TUESDAY PRAYER

Father, I want to control the future.

I want to know what's coming so I can prepare for it. I want certainty so I feel secure. I want guarantees so I don't have to trust.

But that's not faith. That's control.

Teach me to walk into the unknown with confidence. Teach me to trust You with what I can't see. Teach me that uncertainty doesn't mean insecurity when You're the one holding my future.

In Jesus' name, Amen.

WEDNESDAY PRAYER

Lord, help me stop demanding to see before I'll trust.

I've been waiting for clarity about the future before I'll have faith. I've been insisting on knowing what's coming before I'll believe You're good.

But faith doesn't work that way. Faith trusts what it can't see. Faith believes before it knows.

Help me walk into the unknown with confidence in You.

In Jesus' name, Amen.

THURSDAY PRAYER

God, the future is uncertain.

But You're not. You're constant. You're faithful. You're in control.

And that's what I'm anchoring myself in. Not in knowing what's coming, but in knowing who's with me.

You hold my future. And I'm trusting You with it.

In Jesus' name, Amen.

FRIDAY PRAYER

Father, I'm looking ahead with faith.

Not with naive optimism. Not with blind hope. But with trust in You.

I don't know what next year holds. But I know You're good. I know You're working. I know You love me.

And that's enough to walk into the unknown with peace.

In Jesus' name, Amen.

SATURDAY PRAYER

God, I released control this week.

I stopped demanding to know the future. I stopped insisting on certainty. I chose faith over fear.

And it changed how I felt about what's coming. The uncertainty doesn't feel as heavy when I'm trusting You with it.

Help me keep walking this way. Into the unknown with faith, not fear.

In Jesus' name, Amen.

SUNDAY REFLECTION

Reflect:

- What are you afraid of about the future? How does that change if you trust God with it?

- What would it look like to walk into the unknown with faith instead of fear?

Declare:

- I don't know what's coming, but I know who holds my future.

- I will walk into the unknown with faith, not fear.

- God is faithful, even when the path is uncertain.

Carry This: "Now faith is confidence in what we hope for and assurance about what we do not see.", Hebrews 11:1 (NIV)

SUNDAY PRAYER

God, I'm walking into next year with faith.

I don't know what it holds. But I know You're with me. And that's enough.

This week, I learned to trust You with the unknown. To look ahead with confidence, not because the path is clear, but because You're faithful.

The future is uncertain. But You're not. And I'm anchoring myself in that.

In Jesus' name, Amen.

WEEK 52: THE END OF A YEAR, THE BEGINNING OF FOREVER

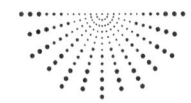

MONDAY DEVOTIONAL

You made it.

Fifty-two weeks. Fifty-two devotionals. Hundreds of prayers. And you're still here.

That's not small. That's faithfulness.

You didn't give up when it got hard. You didn't quit when nothing changed. You kept showing up, kept praying, kept trusting.

And that matters.

Your circumstances might look the same as they did when you started. You might still be single. You might still be waiting. You might still have unanswered questions.

But you're different.

You've grown. You've healed. You've wrestled with God and come out stronger. You've learned what it means to trust Him when nothing makes sense.

And this journey? It's not over.

This is the end of a year. But it's not the end of your story.

Revelation 21:5 says,

> "He who was seated on the throne said, 'I am making everything new!'" (NIV).

Everything new.

Not just some things. Not just what you can see. Everything.

God is still working. He's still writing your story. He's still making all things new.

And whatever comes next, whether it's marriage or continued singleness, whether it's what you hoped for or something completely different, God will be there.

He's been with you through these fifty-two weeks. And He'll be with you through the next fifty-two.

This isn't the end. It's a milestone. A marker of how far you've come and a reminder that there's still more ahead.

So take a breath. Celebrate what God has done. Acknowledge how you've grown.

And then keep going.

Because your story isn't finished. And God isn't done with you yet.

MONDAY PRAYER

God, I made it.

Fifty-two weeks. And I'm still here. Still trusting. Still hoping.

That's because of You. Not because of me.

Thank You for walking with me through this year. Thank You for meeting me in every prayer, every struggle, every moment I thought I couldn't keep going.

I'm different than I was when I started. I've grown. I've healed. I've changed.

And I'm grateful for that. Even if my circumstances haven't changed, I have.

In Jesus' name, Amen.

TUESDAY PRAYER

Father, my circumstances look the same.

I'm still single. I'm still waiting. I'm still hoping for what I don't have yet.

But I'm different. And that's what matters.

Help me celebrate the growth instead of resenting the circumstances. Help me see what's changed in me instead of only focusing on what hasn't changed around me.

You've been working this whole time. And I'm trusting that You're not done yet.

In Jesus' name, Amen.

WEDNESDAY PRAYER

Lord, this is a milestone, not the end.

I've finished fifty-two weeks. But my story isn't finished. My journey isn't over. You're still writing, still working, still making all things new.

Help me see this as a marker of progress, not a conclusion. Help me celebrate how far I've come while still looking ahead with faith.

This is the end of a year. But it's not the end of my story.

In Jesus' name, Amen.

THURSDAY PRAYER

God, I don't know what next year holds.

But I know You'll be there. Just like You were this year.

You walked with me through every hard moment. You sustained me when I thought I couldn't keep going. You gave me strength I didn't have on my own.

And I'm trusting You'll do it again. Whatever comes next, You'll be with me.

In Jesus' name, Amen.

FRIDAY PRAYER

Father, You're making all things new.

Not just some things. Everything.

My story isn't finished. My season isn't over. You're still working, still moving, still writing.

And I'm trusting that whatever comes next, it's part of the new thing You're doing.

In Jesus' name, Amen.

SATURDAY PRAYER

God, I'm celebrating this week.

I finished the year. I grew. I healed. I changed. And I'm grateful for all of it.

But I'm also looking ahead. Because this isn't the end. It's just the beginning of whatever comes next.

You've been faithful through these fifty-two weeks. And I'm trusting You'll be faithful through the next fifty-two.

In Jesus' name, Amen.

SUNDAY REFLECTION

Reflect:

- How are you different than you were fifty-two weeks ago?

- What has God done in you this year that you want to carry forward?

Declare:

- This is the end of a year, not the end of my story.

- God is making all things new, including me.

- I am different, even if my circumstances aren't.

> **Carry This:** "He who was seated on the throne said, 'I am making everything new!'", Revelation 21:5a (NIV)

SUNDAY PRAYER

God, this is the end of a year, but not the end of my story.

I've grown more than I realized. I've healed deeper than I expected. I've changed in ways I couldn't have predicted.

And I'm grateful. For every week. For every prayer. For every moment You met me.

My circumstances might not look different. But I do. And that's what matters.

Thank You for these fifty-two weeks. And thank You for whatever comes next.

You're making all things new. And I'm trusting You with the rest of my story.

In Jesus' name, Amen.

PART II

PART I
CALENDAR HARD DAYS

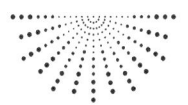

NEW YEAR'S EVE/DAY

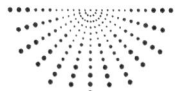

THE "MAYBE THIS YEAR" CYCLE

Another New Year. Another round of "maybe this will be my year." Another list of hopes that may or may not come true.

You're tired of the cycle. Tired of hoping things will change and waking up to the same reality. Tired of watching the calendar flip while your life stays the same.

But new years don't create new realities. God does. And He's been working all along, whether the calendar acknowledges it or not.

Prayer:

God, I'm tired of the "maybe this year" cycle. Tired of pinning my hopes on a date change that doesn't actually change anything.

But I know You're not bound by calendars. You're working in Your timing, not mine. And just because nothing changed when the clock struck midnight doesn't mean nothing is changing.

Help me stop tying my hope to a date and start anchoring it in You. Help me trust that You're moving, even when I can't see it.

This year might look like last year. But I'm different. And You're still working.

In Jesus' name, Amen.

Declaration:

My hope is not in a new year. My hope is in God. He is working, whether the calendar changes or not.

Hold This:

> **"Because of the Lord's great love we are not consumed, for his compassions never fail. They are new every morning; great is your faithfulness.", Lamentations 3:22-23 (NIV)**

YOUR BIRTHDAY

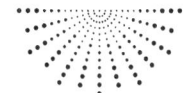

ANOTHER YEAR, STILL SINGLE

Another candle. Another year older. Another birthday where you thought things would be different by now.

You're watching people younger than you get married, have kids, build the life you thought you'd have by this age. And you're wondering if you've somehow missed your window.

You haven't. God's timing doesn't have expiration dates. Your story isn't over just because the timeline didn't go the way you planned.

Prayer:

God, I thought I'd be married by now. I thought my life would look different at this age. And it's hard not to feel like I'm falling behind, like I've somehow failed.

But I know that's not true. Your timing isn't my timing. And just because I'm not where I thought I'd be doesn't mean I'm off track.

Help me celebrate this year for what it is, not resent it for what it's not. Help me trust that You're still writing my story, and the best chapters might still be ahead.

I'm not behind. I'm exactly where You have me.

In Jesus' name, Amen.

Declaration:

My worth is not determined by my age or relationship status. God's timing doesn't have expiration dates. I am exactly where I need to be.

Hold This:

> **"For I know the plans I have for you," declares the Lord, "plans to prosper you and not to harm you, plans to give you hope and a future." , Jeremiah 29:11 (NIV)**

VALENTINE'S DAY

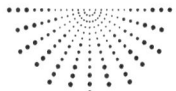

WHEN LOVE IS EVERYWHERE BUT HERE

You woke up to heart-shaped everything. Your coworkers are getting flowers delivered. Your social media is an avalanche of couple photos and romantic gestures. And you're wondering if you're the only person on the planet eating dinner alone tonight.

You're not broken. You're not forgotten. And you're not less loved by God because you don't have romantic love today.

Prayer:

God, today hurts more than most days. I see love celebrated everywhere, and I feel the absence of it in my own life. I don't want to be bitter, but I'm tired of pretending this doesn't sting. Meet me in this loneliness. Remind me that Your love isn't less real because it doesn't come with flowers and chocolate. Help me believe I am fully loved by You, even when I feel unloved by everyone else. Let this day not define my worth.

In Jesus' name, Amen.

Declaration:

I am loved by the God who created love itself. My worth is not measured by relationship status. Today is hard, but it is not my whole story.

Hold This:

> "The Lord appeared to us in the past, saying: 'I have loved you with an everlasting love; I have drawn you with unfailing kindness.'" , Jeremiah 31:3 (NIV)

MOTHER'S DAY/FATHER'S DAY

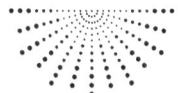

WHEN YOU WANT TO BE A PARENT

MOTHER'S DAY/FATHER'S DAY: When You Want to Be a Parent

Today is for celebrating parents. And you want to be one. But you're not. And you don't know if you ever will be.

You see families everywhere. You hear the tributes, the cards, the flowers. And you feel the ache of a future you're not sure you'll have.

God sees that ache. And He's not ignoring it.

Prayer:

God, I want to be a parent. I want a family. I want to experience the love, the chaos, the joy of raising children.

But I'm not there yet. And I don't know if I ever will be.

That ache is real. And I'm not going to pretend it's not. But I'm also choosing to trust You with it.

If parenthood is part of my story, You'll bring it in Your timing. And if it's not, You'll give me grace to walk a different path.

Either way, I'm trusting You. Even when it hurts.

In Jesus' name, Amen.

Declaration:

My desire for children is not wrong. God sees it, and He's not ignoring it. I trust Him with my future.

Hold This:

> **"Delight yourself in the Lord, and he will give you the desires of your heart.", Psalm 37:4 (NIV)**

WEDDING SEASON

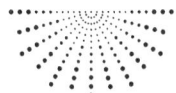

SURVIVING MAY THROUGH SEPTEMBER

Another invitation. Another save-the-date. Another wedding where you'll smile through the ceremony and leave before the bouquet toss.

You're happy for them. You are. But you're also exhausted. Exhausted from celebrating everyone else's love story while yours stays on pause.

Wedding season is hard. And you're allowed to feel that.

Prayer:

God, I'm tired of weddings. Tired of celebrating everyone else's happily ever after while I'm still waiting for mine to start.

I don't want to be bitter. I don't want to resent my friends. But I'm tired. And I don't know how to keep showing up with a smile when it hurts this much.

Help me celebrate genuinely. Help me be present without comparing. Help me trust that their timeline doesn't affect mine.

Their story is theirs. Mine is mine. And You're writing both.

In Jesus' name, Amen.

Declaration:

I can celebrate others without diminishing my own story. Their timeline doesn't dictate mine.

Hold This:

> "Rejoice with those who rejoice; mourn with those who mourn.", Romans 12:15 (NIV)

THANKSGIVING

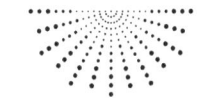

WHEN FAMILY ASKS "THE QUESTION" AGAIN

You knew it was coming. The moment you walked in the door, you knew someone would ask.

"So, are you seeing anyone?"

And now you're sitting at the table, fielding questions about your love life while everyone else talks about their spouse, their kids, their normal lives.

You're grateful for what you have. But you're also tired of being the only single person in the room.

Prayer:

God, I'm tired of the questions. Tired of explaining why I'm still single. Tired of feeling like I'm the family project everyone's trying to fix.

But I don't need fixing. I'm not broken just because I'm single. I'm not less than just because my life looks different.

Help me set boundaries with grace. Help me navigate these conversations without losing my peace. Help me remember that my worth isn't determined by whether I have a plus-one.

I'm grateful for what I have. And I'm trusting You with what I don't.

In Jesus' name, Amen.

Declaration:

I am not a project to fix. I am whole, loved, and exactly where God has me.

Hold This:

> **"Give thanks in all circumstances; for this is God's will for you in Christ Jesus.", 1 Thessalonians 5:18 (NIV)**

CHRISTMAS

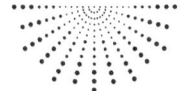

THE EMPTY SEAT AT THE TABLE

Christmas is supposed to be about family. And you have family. But there's still an empty seat where you thought someone would be by now.

Everyone's asking about your love life. Everyone's making jokes about mistletoe. Everyone's assuming you're lonely.

And maybe you are. But that doesn't mean you're less than. It doesn't mean Christmas doesn't belong to you too.

Prayer:

God, Christmas is hard when you're single. The questions. The comments. The assumption that I must be miserable because I'm alone.

But I'm not alone. You're with me. And even though there's an empty seat at the table, that doesn't mean my life is empty.

Help me navigate this season with grace. Help me silence the voices that say I'm less than because I'm single. Help me find joy in what I have instead of only grieving what I don't.

Christmas is Yours. And it's mine too.

In Jesus' name, Amen.

Declaration:

I am not alone, even when I'm single. God is with me. Christmas belongs to me too.

Hold This:

> "Never will I leave you; never will I forsake you.", Hebrews 13:5 (NIV)

PART II
LIFE EVENT HARD DAYS

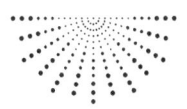

WHEN YOUR EX GETS ENGAGED/MARRIED

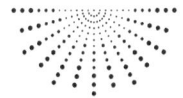

THE MOVING ON THAT BREAKS YOU

You knew it would happen eventually. But knowing doesn't make it easier.

They've moved on. They found someone. They're building the future you thought you'd have together.

And you're still here. Still single. Still wondering what they have that you don't.

Prayer:

God, this hurts more than I expected. Seeing them move on, seeing them happy with someone else, it's breaking something in me I didn't know was still fragile.

I thought I was over it. I thought I'd healed. But this brought it all back.

Help me process this without spiraling. Help me remember that their happiness doesn't mean I'm unlovable. Help me trust that You have something better for me than what I lost.

They're moving on. And I need to keep moving forward too.

In Jesus' name, Amen.

Declaration:

Their moving on doesn't mean I'm left behind. God has a plan for me that's better than what I lost.

Hold This:

> "Forget the former things; do not dwell on the past. See, I am doing a new thing! Now it springs up; do you not perceive it?", Isaiah 43:18-19a (NIV)

WHEN YOUR YOUNGER SIBLING/FRIEND MARRIES FIRST: THE UNEXPECTED STING

You're happy for them. You really are. But you can't shake the feeling that you've been passed over.

They're younger. They've been dating for less time. And now they're getting married while you're still single.

And it doesn't make sense. And it hurts.

Prayer:

God, I didn't expect this to hurt as much as it does. I'm genuinely happy for them. But I also feel left behind.

Why them and not me? What do they have that I don't? Did I do something wrong?

Silence those questions. They're not helpful, and they're not true. Your timing for them is different than Your timing for me. And that's okay.

Help me celebrate without comparing. Help me trust that my story is still being written, even when everyone else's seems to be finishing first.

In Jesus' name, Amen.

Declaration:

God's timing for others doesn't affect His timing for me. I will celebrate without comparing.

Hold This:

> "But each one should test their own actions. Then they can take pride in themselves alone, without comparing themselves to someone else." , Galatians 6:4 (NIV)

AFTER A DEVASTATING BREAKUP: WHEN HOPE JUST DIED

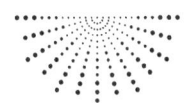

You thought this was it. You really did. You could see the future. You were making plans. You were all in.

And now it's over. And you don't know how to start over again.

Prayer:

God, I'm broken. I thought this was my person. I thought this was finally my time. And now it's over, and I don't know how to recover from this.

I'm angry. I'm hurt. I'm exhausted at the thought of starting over again.

But I know You're with me in this. You see the pieces scattered everywhere. And I'm trusting that You'll help me put them back together.

I don't have the strength to move forward right now. So I'm asking You to carry me until I do.

In Jesus' name, Amen.

Declaration:

This ending is not my ending. God is with me in the wreckage, and He will restore what's broken.

Hold This:

> "The Lord is close to the brokenhearted and saves those who are crushed in spirit.", Psalm 34:18 (NIV)

WHEN YOU'RE THE LAST SINGLE FRIEND: POPULATION: YOU

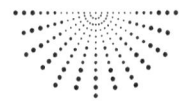

One by one, they all paired off. And now you're the only one left.

You're happy for them. But you're also lonely. Because the dynamic has changed. And you don't fit the same way you used to.

Prayer:

God, I feel so alone. All my friends are married or in relationships. And I'm the only one left.

I'm happy for them. But I also feel forgotten. Left behind. Like I don't belong anymore.

Help me navigate this shift. Help me find new community without resenting the old. Help me trust that You haven't forgotten me just because my friends have moved on.

I'm not less than because I'm the last one single. I'm just on a different timeline.

In Jesus' name, Amen.

Declaration:

Being the last single friend doesn't mean I'm forgotten. God sees me, and He has a plan.

Hold This:

"A friend loves at all times.", Proverbs 17:17a (NIV)

WHEN THE DATES KEEP GOING NOWHERE

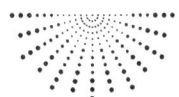

ANOTHER FIRST DATE, ANOTHER DEAD END

You put yourself out there. Again. You tried. Again. You hoped this one might be different.

And it wasn't. Again.

You're tired of first dates that lead nowhere. Tired of investing energy in people who disappear. Tired of hoping for something real and getting nothing.

Prayer:

God, I'm exhausted. I keep trying, and nothing works. I keep putting myself out there, and I keep getting hurt.

I don't know how much more rejection I can take. I don't know how many more dead-end dates I can survive.

But I also don't want to give up. I don't want to close myself off completely.

So I'm asking You to sustain me. To give me hope when I want to quit. To help me keep trying without becoming cynical.

The right person is worth the wait. Help me believe that.

In Jesus' name, Amen.

Declaration:

Failed dates are not wasted time. They're part of the process. The right person is worth the wait.

Hold This:

> "Let us not become weary in doing good, for at the proper time we will reap a harvest if we do not give up.", Galatians 6:9 (NIV)

WHEN YOUR BIOLOGICAL CLOCK IS SCREAMING

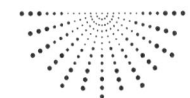

TIME RUNNING OUT

You're not just waiting for love. You're waiting for the chance to be a parent. And time is running out.

Every month that passes feels like a door closing. Every birthday feels like a countdown. And the fear is suffocating.

Prayer:

God, I'm terrified. I want children. I want a family. And I feel like I'm running out of time.

Every month that passes, I feel the window closing. And I don't know what to do with that fear.

But I know You're not bound by biology. I know You're not limited by timelines. I know You can do the impossible.

So I'm trusting You. With my desires. With my timeline. With my future.

If children are part of my story, You'll make it happen. And if they're not, You'll give me grace to walk a different path.

Either way, I'm Yours.

In Jesus' name, Amen.

Declaration:

God is not bound by my biology or my timeline. I trust Him with my future.

Hold This:

"Is anything too hard for the Lord?", Genesis 18:14a (NIV)

CHAPTER ONE

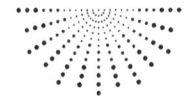

W HEN YOU GET THE "PLUS ONE" INVITATION: Party of One

Another wedding invitation. Another event. Another reminder that the world is designed for couples.

And the dreaded line: "Plus One."

You don't have a plus one. You're going alone. Again.

Prayer:

God, this is such a small thing. But it stings. The assumption that everyone has someone. The awkwardness of showing up alone. The feeling of being the odd one out.

Help me go with confidence. Help me enjoy the event without fixating on who's not beside me. Help me be present instead of feeling sorry for myself.

I'm going alone. But I'm not actually alone. You're with me.

In Jesus' name, Amen.

Declaration:

I don't need a plus one to be complete. I am whole, and God is with me.

Hold This:

"The Lord himself goes before you and will be with you; he will never leave you nor forsake you.", Deuteronomy 31:8a (NIV)

CHAPTER TWO

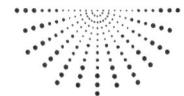

T HE NIGHT LONELINESS FEELS UNBEARABLE: 2 AM and Drowning

It's 2 a.m. The house is quiet. And the loneliness is crushing you.

You can't sleep. You can't think straight. You just ache. For companionship. For someone to be here. For someone to care.

And the silence is deafening.

Prayer:

God, I'm drowning in loneliness right now. The ache is so strong I can barely breathe.

I need You to meet me here. I need to feel Your presence in this silence. I need to know I'm not actually alone, even when it feels like I am.

Be with me in this moment. Comfort me. Remind me that You see me, that You're here, that I matter to You.

I can't fix this loneliness tonight. But I can make it through with You.

In Jesus' name, Amen.

Declaration:

I am not alone. God is with me, even at 2 a.m. His presence is enough.

Hold This:

"Where can I go from your Spirit? Where can I flee from your presence? If I go up to the heavens, you are there; if I make my bed in the depths, you are there.", Psalm 139:7-8 (NIV)

WHEN YOU'RE TIRED OF PRAYING

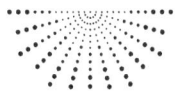

THE WORDS WON'T COME ANYMORE

You've prayed this prayer so many times you've run out of language for it.

You've cried about it. Fasted about it. Journaled about it. Let people speak into it. Released it. Picked it back up. Released it again.

And now you're just tired.

Not rebellious. Not faithless. Just worn out from carrying the same request for so long with no visible change.

You're tired of asking God for something that feels like it's never coming.

You're tired of believing for something you can't see.

You're tired of caring about something that hurts you every time you think about it.

You're tired of praying , not because you don't love God, but because you're out of strength.

And here's the part nobody says out loud:

Sometimes prayer isn't a beautiful, poetic conversation. Sometimes it's survival. Sometimes it's groans. Sometimes it's silence. Sometimes it's nothing.

God isn't offended by that.

God isn't disappointed in you.

God isn't keeping score of how many days you couldn't bring yourself to pray about it again.

He knows the difference between spiritual laziness and spiritual exhaustion. And what you're feeling right now? It's not laziness.

It's the weight of hope deferred.

And God meets you even here. Especially here.

Prayer:

God, I don't know what to say anymore. I've prayed every version of this prayer. The words feel recycled, empty, and worn out.

I'm tired of hoping. Tired of believing. Tired of asking for something that never seems to change.

I don't feel strong. I don't feel spiritual. I don't feel full of faith.

But I'm still Yours. And I still need You.

If I can't pray right now, let my silence count as a prayer. If I can't form the words, let my tears be enough. If I'm too tired to hope, hold the hope for me.

Meet me in this exhaustion. Intercede for me when I can't intercede for myself. Carry this request when I'm too weak to keep lifting it.

Give me enough strength for one more day. One more step. One more whisper of trust.

Because You're still God, even when I'm tired. And I'm still trying, even when I don't have the words.

In Jesus' name, Amen.

Declaration:

Being tired doesn't mean I've lost faith. My silence isn't failure , it's surrender. God hears even the prayers I'm too exhausted to speak.

Hold This:

> "In the same way, the Spirit helps us in our weakness. We do not know what we ought to pray for, but the Spirit himself intercedes for us through wordless groans.", Romans 8:26 (NIV)

PART III
CHURCH & COMMUNITY HARD DAYS

WHEN CHURCH FEELS LIKE COUPLES CLUB

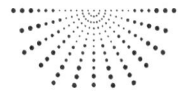

INVISIBLE IN GOD'S HOUSE

You walk into church and it's couples everywhere. Holding hands. Sitting together. Serving together.

And you feel invisible. Like church was designed for families and you're just tolerated.

You want to belong. But you don't know where you fit.

Prayer:

God, church is hard when you're single. I feel like I don't fit. Like everything is designed for families and I'm just an afterthought.

But I know that's not true. I know Your church is for everyone. I know I belong, even if it doesn't feel like it.

Help me find my place. Help me connect with people who see me. Help me remember that my value in the body of Christ isn't tied to my relationship status.

I belong here. Help me believe that.

In Jesus' name, Amen.

Declaration:

I belong in the church. My value is not determined by my relationship status.

Hold This:

> "Now you are the body of Christ, and each one of you is a part of it.",
> 1 Corinthians 12:27 (NIV)

WHEN SOMEONE SAYS "YOU'RE TOO PICKY"

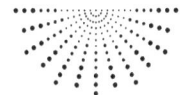

DEFENDING YOUR STANDARDS

Someone just told you you're too picky. That you need to lower your standards. That you're never going to find anyone if you keep being so particular. And for a moment, their words get in your head. You start wondering if they're seeing something you can't. You start questioning whether your expectations are the problem. You start thinking maybe you're asking for too much.

But you're not. Wanting someone healthy, stable, respectful, aligned with your values, consistent in their actions, and emotionally mature is not being too picky. It's being wise. And sometimes people call you picky because you refuse to settle for chaos, confusion, or crumbs. Your standards aren't the issue—they're the boundary that protects your heart.

PRAYER:

God, I'm second-guessing myself. Maybe I am too picky. Maybe my standards are too high. Maybe I'm the problem. But I know that wanting someone who shares my values, treats me well, and is emotionally healthy is not asking for too much. It's wanting a relationship that honors You and honors me. Help me hold my standards without apologizing. Help me trust that desiring a healthy, aligned relationship is not unreasonable. Strengthen my confidence so I don't shrink myself to fit someone who isn't good for me. I'm not settling. I'm waiting for what's right.

In Jesus' name, Amen.

Declaration:

Having standards is wisdom, not pickiness. I will not settle for less than what is healthy.

Hold This:

> "Above all else, guard your heart, for everything you do flows from it.", Proverbs 4:23 (NIV)

WHEN SOMEONE SAYS "JUST TRUST GOD'S TIMING"

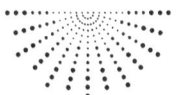

WHEN PLATITUDES PIERCE

You've heard it a thousand times. "Just trust God's timing." "It'll happen when you least expect it." "God's plan is perfect."

You know people mean well. You know they're trying to encourage you. But it doesn't help. Not when you're the one living the waiting. Not when they've never had to carry what you're carrying. Instead of comfort, it leaves you feeling misunderstood and even more alone.

Because the waiting is real. The ache is real. And simple phrases don't touch deep pain. They feel dismissive. They make it seem like your struggle should be solved with a sentence. And when it isn't, you start wondering if your faith is the problem.

People who never waited this long tell you to "be patient." People who've never felt this kind of loneliness tell you to "just trust God." They don't understand the weight behind those words.

PRAYER:

God, I'm tired of the platitudes. Tired of hearing easy answers from people who haven't walked this path. I am trusting You, but that doesn't make this season easy. And quick phrases don't make it better.

Help me give grace to people who don't understand. Help me release the frustration I feel when their words miss the mark. Bring people into my life who can sit with me, listen, and understand. Remind me that I can trust You and still admit that this is hard.

In Jesus' name, Amen.

DECLARATION:

Trusting God's timing doesn't mean the waiting is easy. I can trust and struggle at the same time.

Hold This:

> "Trust in the Lord with all your heart and lean not on your own understanding.", Proverbs 3:5 (NIV)

WHEN SEXUAL TEMPTATION OVERWHELMS

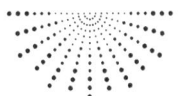

THE STRUGGLE NO ONE TALKS ABOUT

You're trying to honor God with your body. You're fighting for purity. But right now, the temptation is overwhelming.

And you feel like you're the only one struggling with this.

You're not.

Prayer:

God, I'm struggling. The temptation is so strong right now, and I don't know how to fight it.

I want to honor You with my body. I want to live in purity. But I'm weak. And I need Your help.

Give me strength to resist. Give me the courage to flee. Give me people I can be honest with about this struggle.

I can't do this alone. But with You, I can make it through this moment.

In Jesus' name, Amen.

Declaration:

Sexual temptation is not sin. I am not alone in this struggle. God gives me strength to resist.

Hold This:

"No temptation has overtaken you except what is common to mankind. And God is faithful; he will not let you be tempted beyond what you can bear.", 1 Corinthians 10:13a (NIV)

WHEN YOU WONDER IF SOMETHING'S WRONG WITH YOU

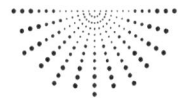

THE CORE FEAR

Everyone else is finding someone. Everyone else is getting chosen. Everyone else is moving forward.

And you're still here. Still single. Still wondering why it hasn't happened for you yet. Still fighting the quiet fear that you're being left behind.

You tell yourself you're fine, but deep down, you're tired of being the one who keeps showing up alone. You're tired of being strong. You're tired of pretending it doesn't bother you.

And in the middle of all of that, the question slips in: *"What's wrong with me?"*

PRAYER:

God, I'm afraid something is fundamentally wrong with me. That I'm unlovable. That I'm too broken, too difficult, too much for anyone to want.

And I know that's not true. But some days, I believe it anyway.

Silence that lie. Remind me that my worth isn't determined by whether someone chooses me. Remind me that I am loved, valued, and seen by You.

Help me trust that I'm not behind—I'm just on a different timeline. Remind me that waiting doesn't mean something is wrong with me; it means You're writing my story in a different way.

In Jesus' name, Amen.

DECLARATION:

There is nothing wrong with me. I am loved, valued, and chosen by God.

HOLD THIS:

> "I praise you because I am fearfully and wonderfully made; your works are wonderful, I know that full well.", Psalm 139:14 (NIV)

ABOUT THE AUTHOR

ABOUT THE MIND OF MALACHI

The Mind of Malachi is a contemplative collective shaped by those who live between promise and fulfillment. A gathering of voices, stories, prayers, and melodies that refuse to settle for shallow optimism.

Born from a desire to speak honestly to the weary, the overlooked, and the spiritually hungry, The Mind of Malachi blends faith, poetry, and raw truth into expressions that meet believers in the tension.

This collective is the creative home behind The Griot, the debut musical experience that confronts faith, identity, struggle, and hope with fearless vulnerability, and now Between Now and Not Yet, a year-long devotional journey crafted for believers navigating seasons of waiting, longing, and becoming.

More than an author name, The Mind of Malachi is a posture:

A willingness to wrestle with God. A refusal to fake faith. A commitment to speak truth with compassion. A belief that God meets us, fully, in the in-between.

instagram.com/themindofmalachi
facebook.com/themindofmalachi
tiktok.com/@themindofmalachi

ALSO BY THE MIND OF MALACHI

MUSIC BY THE MIND OF MALACHI

THE GRIOT — A Lyrical Bible Study Experience (Music)
Featuring *Waiting for You,* the inspiration behind this devotional for singles.

ACKNOWLEDGMENTS

To everyone living in the tension between what God promised and what you see, this book is for you.

To the ones who wait, not passively, but faithfully. You are the heartbeat of this message.

To every believer who refuses to fake a smile just to appear spiritual, thank you for your honesty.

To every friend who shared their story, their pain, or their prayers, your vulnerability shaped these pages.

To the communities who have embraced The Mind of Malachi, your hunger for truth, your courage, and your devotion continue to breathe life into this work.

And most of all, to the God who meets us in the wait. Thank You for never leaving us in-between.

SCRIPTURE CREDITS

Unless otherwise indicated, all Scripture quotations are taken from the Holy Bible, New International Version®, NIV®. Copyright © 1973, 1978, 1984, 2011 by Biblica, Inc.™ Used by permission of Zondervan. All rights reserved worldwide. www.zondervan.com. The "NIV" and "New International Version" are trademarks registered in the United States Patent and Trademark Office by Biblica, Inc.™

A FINAL BLESSING

May God meet you in the in-between.

May you feel seen in the waiting, strengthened in the wondering, and held in the places that ache.

You are not behind. You are not overlooked. You are not forgotten.

Your "not yet" is not a denial. It is preparation.

And even here. Even now. God is with you.

.

www.ingramcontent.com/pod-product-compliance
Lightning Source LLC
Chambersburg PA
CBHW070527090426
42735CB00013B/2882